Baton Basics

Baton Basics

Communicating Music through Gestures

DIANE WITTRY

OXFORD
UNIVERSITY PRESS

OXFORD
UNIVERSITY PRESS

Oxford University Press is a department of the University of
Oxford. It furthers the University's objective of excellence in research,
scholarship, and education by publishing worldwide.

Oxford   New York
Auckland   Cape Town   Dar es Salaam   Hong Kong   Karachi
Kuala Lumpur   Madrid   Melbourne   Mexico City   Nairobi
New Delhi   Shanghai   Taipei   Toronto

With offices in
Argentina   Austria   Brazil   Chile   Czech Republic   France   Greece
Guatemala   Hungary   Italy   Japan   Poland   Portugal   Singapore
South Korea   Switzerland   Thailand   Turkey   Ukraine   Vietnam

Oxford is a registered trademark of Oxford University Press
in the UK and certain other countries.

Published in the United States of America by
Oxford University Press
198 Madison Avenue, New York, NY 10016

Library of Congress Cataloging-in-Publication Data
Wittry, Diane, author.
Baton basics : communicating music through gestures / Diane Wittry.
  pages cm
  Includes bibliographical references and index.
ISBN 978-0-19-935415-3 (hardcover : alk. paper) — ISBN 978-0-19-935416-0 (pbk. : alk. paper)
1. Conducting—Instruction and study.   I. Title.
MT85.W66 2014
781.45—dc23
2014003344

CONTENTS

I would like to dedicate this book to all the students who have taken my Beyond the Baton Conducting Workshops and Seminars. I have learned so much from working with all of you!

Special thanks to Joseph Gifford for opening my eyes to a new way of looking at body movement and the communication of energy, and to Rick Peckham for creating all the illustrations, conducting diagrams, and the companion videos for this book.

Conducting

The art of shaping, guiding, and inspiring a musical idea through body gesture.

Gesture

The use of motion of the arms and body as a means of expression that emphasizes an idea, sentiment, emotion, or attitude.

Inspiration

The action or power of influencing the emotions or intellect of others in a creative, stimulating way.

ABOUT THE COMPANION WEBSITE

www.oup.com/us/batonbasics

We are pleased to announce that there will be a Companion Website for *Baton Basics—Communicating Music Through Gestures*. This website will feature over 60 videos of the conducting exercises in the book. Each of these video examples is marked in the book with this symbol (▶). Some of the videos are listed in text boxes that include all of the examples in that specific video. As you read through *Baton Basics*, you can refer to these videos for clarification of all of the exercises. Watching these videos should make everything easier to understand throughout the book and will give you a model that enhances the learning process. Special thanks and appreciation goes to Reuben Blundell, Gemma New, and Michael Avagliano for their participation in these conducting videos.

Baton Basics

Introduction

When I began conducting, I was a junior in college. Conducting was a required course for all music majors, and I was very excited about learning how to communicate musical ideas to a group of musicians. As the course began, I was how told to hold a baton, and to stretch out my right arm parallel to the floor. I was then given some specific diagrams to follow regarding how to beat patterns of 1, 2, 3, 4, and 6.

My arms were long, my elbows stuck out. I did not know how to stand. I puzzled over what to do with my feet, arms, and shoulders. My wrist flopped up and down and I bounced and bent my knees, but I was *conducting*. After a while, with practice, I perfected the timing of giving cues, beating larger for "forte" and smaller for "piano," faster for "allegro" and slower for "adagio." For "legato," I connected the beat more, and for "staccato," I used a sharper, clearer beat.

Years later, though, I looked back on my initial training and wondered what the results would have been if I had started out from a different place. What if I could have actually developed the specific conducting technique and diverse muscle memory training that would have allowed me to communicate musical ideas through gestures on infinitely more levels?

Over the years, as I strove to become a better musician and a better conductor, I began to realize that the conducting field, unlike the training for violin or other instruments, is not as defined regarding the teaching of conducting technique. Various conducting teachers utilize different approaches regarding where the beat is placed, how much "ictus" or "rhythmic stress" is used, how one uses gesture to affect the quality of the sound, and how each conductor communicates with his or her ensemble. With some investigation, a few schools of thought surfaced with distinct approaches to conducting gestures.

Early on, everyone followed the philosophy and the famous conducting diagrams of the great German conductor Max Rudolph in his classic book, *The Grammar of Conducting*. More recently, many well-known Russian conductors were trained in techniques developed by the conducting teacher Ilya Musin from the Saint Petersburg Conservatory. In Japan, the Hideo Saito conducting method was utilized by many respected conductors, including Seiji Ozawa. Across the United States, young conductors were infatuated with, and greatly influenced by, Leonard Bernstein's enthusiastic style; by Robert Shaw's emphasis on ensemble tone color; and by the clear, precise technique and gestures of the conductors for our fine military bands.

In studying all of these methods, I found that a variety of gestures and techniques could be identified that were effective in communicating the essence of the music to the musicians. From these approaches, I set out to develop a series of finger, hand, wrist, forearm, and full arm exercises that would enable conductors to increase their vocabulary of gestures, strengthen their muscles, and better align their bodies so that musical energy would flow more freely through the conductor, out to the musicians, and ultimately to the audience.

If you are new to conducting, no longer will you feel limited in your beat patterns, or be confined to simply beating with "legato" or "staccato" motions. If you have been conducting for years, you will be able to integrate these new ideas into your current repertoire of gestures. Being knowledgeable about a large variety of gestures, training your muscles to replicate them, and understanding which motion to use at a given point in the music are all valuable to making great music with an ensemble.

It is my goal that this book will help people of all body types become more familiar and connected with how their bodies work for them as conductors. I will show you ways to change your overall posture in order to reduce your physical stress, and I will methodically take you through exercises to develop a larger vocabulary of conducting gestures. Finally, we will explore concepts of relaxing and controlling your mind so that you can mentally go into a different "zone" to access more energy and inspiration.

The art of conducting takes a lifetime to master. No matter how musically intelligent you are, if you do not have a vocabulary of gestures to communicate your musical ideas to your ensemble, you will not succeed as a conductor. This book should introduce you to new motions and gesture concepts that will enable you to take your conducting technique to a new level. I hope that this book will change the way you think about beat patterns and that it will give you better tools to communicate your musical ideas in order to create inspired performances.

Diane Wittry

The Body

Conducting an ensemble requires a person to communicate a uniform message to a group of musicians through organized gestures in order to inspire the performance of a musical idea or concept. The ability of the individual to convey this message through clear and diverse body gestures greatly influences that person's success as a conductor. Of course, it is possible simply to beat time and the ensemble will usually play together, but the role of the conductor goes far beyond being a time-keeper. Developing a vocabulary of varied gestures and understanding their effective applications is critically important for any serious conductor. Simply knowing the placement of the beats 1, 2, 3, 4 is just the beginning of your lifelong study of the art form. Beyond that, you must train your entire body, almost the same way that a ballet dancer trains, so that your body is always working "for" you in helping you to communicate with your musical group. Never should your posture or gestures block your energy or send mixed signals to the musicians. Developing a relaxed, open stance and a deeper understanding of body gestures will help ensure your success as a conductor.

In order to be an excellent conductor, you have to spend some time actually training your muscles. There are physical requirements for standing for long periods of time and for moving your arms and shoulders without straining them. If you are conducting with tension, you will eventually develop back and shoulder problems that may keep you from continuing as a conductor. Beyond that, conducting with tension creates a stressful musical performance and conflicts with the concept of inspiring your musicians to perform their best.

Most people do not spend enough time understanding how the muscles of their bodies affect their conducting. Many conductors are all too eager to start waving their arms in the conducting patterns defined in most conducting textbooks. Conducting, however, is not about beating time. There are conductors out there who never beat in a precise pattern and yet inspire exquisite music. Conducting is about communicating emotion, character, intensity, and mood to a large group of musicians, within a defined tempo, in order to inspire them to create music together. It is a team effort. As a conductor, you will never make any sound. You are totally dependent on the musicians in front of you for the quality of the music making. The way you inspire, motivate, and guide these performers will define the audience's listening experience. Refining your means of communication through gestures will greatly enhance your ability to produce inspired performances.

One of the unique things about each of us is that we have different body configurations. Some people have short torsos; others have very long arms. Some are thin with small bone structure, and thus may have difficulty displaying a commanding presence on the podium; others are quite stout and might have problems moving quickly and lightly. Having long arms and bony elbows can often impede communication of the fullness of the phrase; and how a person holds their head, chin, and shoulders is critical for keeping the energy flowing and allowing the music to breathe.

We cannot easily change the body that we have. Therefore, we must explore and perfect the most effective motions for our particular body type. We must also learn to align and strengthen all the muscles involved with conducting gestures, so that these muscles will work smoothly for us without tension as we develop our conducting technique.

GETTING STARTED

For you to conduct correctly, your entire body must be aligned and relaxed. Tension anywhere will interfere with the music making and will eventually create physical problems. To establish a correct position for avoiding tension in your body, we will start with the feet and work our way up to the top of the head. The following exercises explore ways to create the proper alignment position for your body when conducting.

THE CONDUCTING SPACE

As you prepare to practice conducting, chose a space that gives you enough room to move about. The room should be large enough for you to look around and envision your imaginary orchestra, band, or chorus. Map out an imaginary podium space of about four square feet. Make sure that you have enough light in your work area. You will need a music stand for some of the exercises but it is not critical at the beginning. Usually a solid Manhasset music stand is best because you can adjust the angle and it is very sturdy.

When starting out, do not use a space with a mirror, even though you may want to see how your gestures look. A mirror tends to inhibit your movements and shifts your focus from your hands to your eyes, thus you develop a habit of conducting with your eyes and face while sending a separate message through your hands. The goal is to communicate through one focal point: your hand, if you are a choral conductor; and the tip of your baton, if you are an instrumental conductor.

Entering the Conducting Space

Entering your conducting space is like stepping on to the podium. Your ensemble will begin to judge you subconsciously and to respond to you from the moment you walk into the room. This simple act, which we often take for granted—the manner in which you walk to the podium and stand on it—can greatly influence your effectiveness as a conductor. Practice walking across the room into your conducting space. As you walk, keep your head high, shoulders relaxed and down. Walk with confidence. You may want to videorecord yourself walking into your conducting space.

When you watch the recording, analyze the way you would react to yourself if you were a member of the ensemble. Practice this until you feel you are portraying warmth and confidence in the way you enter the room. Be confident, but not arrogant; friendly and open, but not gushy or false; relaxed, but strong at the same time. Become the type of musical leader that people can believe in and would like to follow.

As you walk to your imaginary podium, collect your thoughts and center your energy. Focus your mind on the music that you are going to conduct. Walk past everything else as if it does not exist. Only one thing in the world is important and real at that moment: the music, and the way you are going to communicate this music to the group before you.

BODY POSTURE

Most of us have been standing on our feet since the age of two, or longer, and because we have been doing it so long, we assume that we know how to stand correctly. Standing in one place for a long time, relaxed without tension, is not as easy as it first seems. Over the years, one can unconsciously develop habits of slouching, leaning to one side, or standing with tension in our muscles. After a while, this tension in our bodies becomes second nature and we do not even realize we are stressed.

As you practice standing in one place, see if you can identify areas of tension in your body. Is your head or neck tight? Are you carrying stress in your shoulders? Are you able to balance your weight evenly between your feet, or is one leg holding more weight than the other? Is there tension in your lower back? Can you release this tension? The following concepts will help you address these issues.

Imaginary String

As you are standing, imagine that there is a string coming out of the very top of your head. It is pulling your body upward. The string comes up through your backbone and neck and out through the top of your head, pulling your head upward through the neck vertebrae, but keeping the chin down, close to your chest. Feel your body as it is being lifted and stretched by the pull of the string. Your neck and back vertebrae extend upward as your shoulders remain low and relaxed. At the same time, your feet should feel heavy and grounded. It is the extension between the grounding of your feet and the lifting of the head and torso that creates a space for the circulation of energy.

THE FEET

As you step up on your imaginary podium, you might wonder what you should do with your feet. In general, when you are conducting, your feet should be planted in one place and they should not move. It is important when you are using a music stand, to place the stand within easy reach to enable you to turn the pages of your score without ever having to

> **The Feet**
> - Feet Placement Chart
> - Weight Shifts
> - Ankle Rotations
>
> **Video 1.1**

move your feet. We have all seen conductors who become "pacers" as they move up to turn a page of the score, then move back to conduct. This extraneous movement becomes distracting. Avoid developing this bad habit from the beginning by being very careful about your music stand placement in relationship to the position of your feet.

When you position your feet, you should always distribute your body weight equally on both of them. Many conductors make the mistake of shifting their weight back and forth, or, even worse, keeping all their weight on only one foot. This type of posture can make it difficult to communicate the strength of the music because you are off-balance and not grounded. Here are some tools and exercises for creating proper placement of your feet and equal weight distribution.

Feet Placement Chart

Even though this exercise sounds very basic, I encourage you to take an 11" × 17" piece of paper and place it on the floor with the 11" side parallel to your feet. Stand on the paper with your feet spread apart at about the same width as your hips. You can have your feet pointed slightly to each side. Now, lean down and draw an outline around your feet. You now have a foot-placement chart. The value in having a chart to stand on is that it will remind you not to move your feet while conducting.

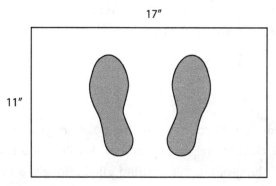

17"

11"

Now place this piece of paper in the center of your imaginary four-foot-square podium space and stand there. Position the music stand in front of you so that you can turn pages without moving your feet off the paper. Memorize the distance that the base of the music stand needs to be from your foot diagram to allow you to comfortably turn the pages. Adjust the height of the music stand so that you do not have to lean over to reach the score. You should be able to reach down and touch the stand without bending your knees or moving your feet. Excessive movement of the feet and body caused by turning the pages of the music when the stand is too far away is one of the core mistakes that beginning conductors make. Each time you practice conducting, use this foot placement chart until your relationship to the music stand becomes second nature.

Shoes

The types of shoes you wear as a conductor will definitely affect your ability to feel grounded and connected. This is especially difficult for women because of the pressure to wear high heels. Flat shoes will make you to feel much more balanced and comfortable, enabling you to stand without tension for long periods of time. Make sure that your shoes are wide enough that your toes can spread out and not be cramped together. Experiment with wearing different types of shoes while you practice conducting. How do you feel when you conduct barefoot compared to when you wear dress shoes? The freer your foot feels, the easier it is for your body to become completely relaxed. Try to find shoes that help you to stay grounded while you are conducting.

Weight Shifts

As you are standing in your conducting position, gradually lean to one side and shift all your weight to that foot. While doing this, leave your other foot on the ground, but position all the weight on the first foot. Count to ten, then shift the weight to the other foot and repeat the exercise. When you have done this with both feet, return to an equal distribution of weight between your feet. Take a minute to focus on the connection of your feet to the ground.

Now, practice shifting the weight from the balls of your feet to your heels, then back to a centered position. Do this a few times until you feel the differences in this weight distribution. For conducting, you want to rest your weight slightly forward on the balls of your feet. Memorize this feeling of balance.

Ankle Rotations

As you stand with your weight balanced on both of your feet, gradually shift the weight to one foot and slowly lift and rotate the other foot in air. Rotate the ankle three or four times, then shake and wiggle the foot vigorously. When finished, place your foot back on the ground in the proper position and adjust your weight equally between your feet again. Practice this same exercise rotating the ankle of your other foot. Develop the skill of being able to balance on either foot without having to hold on to anything for support. A good sense of balance will enable you to release tension and to be more relaxed as you are standing.

GROUNDING THE LOWER BODY

Now, let's concentrate on the rest of your body. Each body part must be in its proper alignment or you will be blocking your musical energy. It is important that your legs and hips are relaxed and grounded. These exercises will release tension from your lower body and help you to feel more centered.

> **Grounding the Lower Body**
>
> • Tiptoes Up and Down
>
> • Leg Kicks
>
> • Leg Swings
>
> • Jump in Place
>
> • Knee Bends
>
> • Sit, Then Stand
>
> **Video 1.2**

Tiptoes Up and Down

Stand with your feet evenly spaced in the proper position, then rise up on your toes for five seconds, and return to flat feet again. Feel your weight become more centered and your body more lifted and relaxed. It seems quite simple, but it is a wonderful way to align your body and release tension. Breathe deeply while doing this and see if you can sense a tingling at the top of your head.

Leg Kicks

Balance your weight on one foot while lifting the other foot in front of you and kicking it forward from the knee as if you were kicking a Hacky Sack or a soccer ball. Kick forward about 16 times. Then place your foot on the ground again and re-center your weight. You should be able to do this without holding on to anything. Repeat the exercise with the other foot. Each time you return your feet to the floor, stand quietly for a few moments so you can feel the release of the tension in your legs and hips.

Leg Swings

Move to a place in the room where you can hold on to the back of a chair with one hand, or place your hand on a table or wall for support. Lift the opposite leg and swing it forward and back like a pendulum. Give it a really good swing. Let it swing freely forward and backward about 16 times, then put the foot back on the floor. This swinging motion will release the muscles around the hip joint. Stand quietly now for about 10 counts and imagine the stress in your legs flowing downward and becoming absorbed into the earth. Then reverse your position and do these pendulum swings with the opposite leg while holding on with the other hand.

Jump in Place

From your standing position, bend your knees slightly so that you can jump up and down in place 10 times. After jumping, reposition your feet with your weight equally distributed and notice how your body feels. Your feet and legs should feel heavier and more solidly connected to the earth. This exercise can be done regularly in your dressing room or back stage right before each concert to quickly ground your body when you are nervous.

Knee Bends

Sometime you are not able to actually jump up and down, but you can achieve a similar result if you simply bend your knees and then stand up again. By bending your knees, you are focusing the weight more purposefully on the soles of your feet. As you do this, keep your back straight and your arms by your sides.

Sit, Then Stand

Another grounding exercise can be done by sitting on the edge of a chair with your back straight. Be sure that your feet are positioned apart, similar to your standing conducting position. Now stand up. Feel how the weight shifts. When you are seated, your lower torso is completely relaxed and grounded on the chair. On standing, you should still feel grounded, except that your body weight will be suddenly shifted to your feet. Repeat this exercise a few times. Memorize how your rooted your body feels when you are seated and try to achieve the same feeling when you are standing.

Now, while you are doing this exercise, move your arms as though you are conducting. Start from a seated position and conduct some basic patterns. When you are comfortable, stand up and continue conducting. After conducting in a standing position for a few moments, sit again and repeat the process. Experience this connection of your lower body to the ground every time you conduct.

THE WAIST AND THE BACK

While your lower body from the hips down must feel like your natural weight is pulling downward, at the same time, your waist, back, and head, must always feel light, buoyant, flexible, and full of energy. It is difficult to achieve this combination. The following exercises will help you train your muscles so that eventually this type of posture will be second nature for you.

> **The Waist and The Back**
>
> • Waist Swivels
> • Side Bends
> • Tai Chi Back Alignment
> • Releasing the Lower Back
> • Flat on the Floor
>
> **Video 1.3** ▶

Waist Swivels

From a standing position with your weight equal on both feet and your arms relaxed at your sides, rotate your hips and turn at the waist to spin your shoulders to each side. This creates a "swivel" movement. Your feet and legs should be stable without movement while your hips and waist should feel grounded but should rotate flexibly. Allow this spinning motion to swing your arms slightly, one in front of and one behind your body. Your arms can slap softly against your body as you turn. Your head should follow your shoulder motion, so that it is also turning right, then left. Perform this exercise about 10 times to loosen the muscles around the hips and waist.

Side Bends

With your hands hanging by your sides, imagine that one hand is tied to a very heavy bowling ball. Experience that bowling ball pulling down on your hand and arm. Feel the release at the shoulder as the weight of the bowling ball causes a slight bending sideways at the waist. As the side with the heavy bowling ball bends, the other side of your waist will stretch and expand.

It is important to reverse this exercise so that you release both sides of your body. Imagine the bowling ball is now attached to the other hand. Feel the stretch in the other side of your waist and the release of tension in your shoulder as the bowling ball pulls your hand downward.

Now, place both of your hands on your hips and gradually bend sideways at the waist, lowering your shoulder to one side. Hold that position for a few seconds and then slowly return to center. Inhale and exhale deeply before doing the same motion to the other side. Feel the muscles on each side of your waist extend, stretch, and relax.

Buttocks Squeeze

While you are standing with your weight balanced on both feet, tighten the muscles of your buttocks, hold for 10 seconds, then release. Repeat a few times. Each time you do this, try to release more tension. Keep your upper body relaxed and your rib cage lifted as you perform this exercise. Most of us tend to carry tension in our lower back. This exercise can gently help release this stress.

Back Bend and Vertebrae Alignment

Many conductors suffer from back problems that are caused by conducting with tension. This is something you really want to avoid. To properly align the back vertebrae, the following Tai chi exercise is helpful.

Releasing the Back

Slowly bend your head down until your chin touches your chest, then continue to bend each vertebra downward, like a pill-bug slowly rolling up. In your final position, your head will be down at your knees, with your hair hanging toward the floor. Your knees should be slightly bent and the arms hanging down loosely, almost touching your toes. Shake your arms gently while you breathe in and exhale slowly.

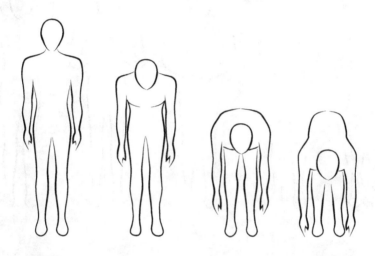

Releasing More Tension

Now, extend your arms even further toward the floor, wiggling them from your shoulders and allowing them to flop around. Feel the dead weight of your arms where everything is very loose. Gradually turn your head, rolling it slowly in both directions to loosen it at the neck. Then, loosen the muscles in your back where your hips connect to the lower back by turning your body slightly back and forth and adjusting your hips.

Coming Back Up

When you are totally relaxed, you can start coming up again. Move your hands together so that your fingers are lightly touching each other. As you rise, begin from the lower back and gradually straighten each vertebra, allowing them to stack on top of each other, while the head and arms follow. Keep your head down with your arms hanging loosely as long as possible. As your shoulders finally come up and roll back, allow your hands to continue upward, tracing the center of your body until you are lifting your arms, fingers still touching, high over your head.

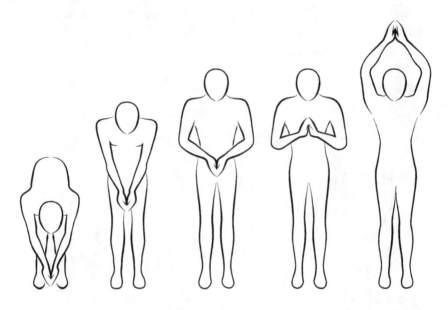

IMAGINARY SHOWER

After your arms and hands have formed a pencil point above your head, you can gradually lift your chin and tilt your head upward with your eyes looking toward your hands and the ceiling. Now, turn the palms of your hands outward and move them in opposite directions out to each side of your body and then gradually downward. As you slowly move your arms down, imagine a shower of water lightly cascading onto your head and washing over your body. Feel the weight of the water as it pulls your arms and shoulders down. When your arms reach your sides, drop your chin back onto your chest and begin the exercise again. Repeat this exercise about 10 times. After you complete the last repetition, rest for a moment and see if you experience a tingling at the top of your head and more energy flowing through your body.

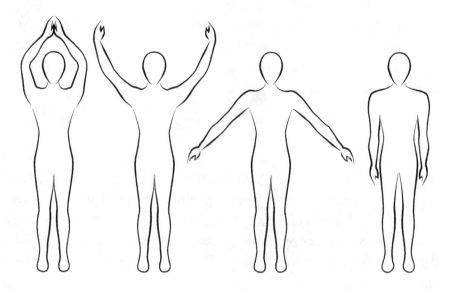

Releasing the Lower Back

Lie down on the floor on your back with your arms at your sides, then bend both knees and bring them up to your chest. Encircle your knees with your arms and rock gently back and forth on your back. Roll your body to the right and then to the left, letting your head roll in the same direction with your body. Hold your position on each side for a few counts before you return to the center. As you draw your knees closer to your chest, feel the pull in your lower back as it stretches and extends.

When you have finished, gradually move your legs down so that your knees are still bent but your feet are now flat on the floor. Feel how your lower back is more relaxed and connected to the floor than when you began. Hold this position for a few minute as you adjust your hips to release the lower back even more. If you are still experiencing tension try squeezing and releasing your buttocks a few times.

When you are completely relaxed, move your legs down flat so that your entire body is resting on the floor. Remain here breathing deeply for a few minutes as you imagine all your tension flowing into the floor beneath you.

Flat on the Floor

As you lie on your back with your hands folded over your stomach, feel the weight of your body relax into the ground. Imagine that a magnet in the earth is pulling all of the negative energy out of your body. Open up your chest and rib cage by releasing your shoulders so that they are also flat, touching the floor. Breathe deeply and focus on the expansion of your chest and rib cage.

Stand against a Wall

Now, slowly stand up and try to recreate the relaxed, grounded feeling of lying on the floor as you move to stand with your back against a wall. Adjust your shoulders backwards until they are touching the wall, which will open up your chest. Your head should be slightly forward from the wall about two inches and you should keep your chin down.

From this position, experiment with conducting basic patterns. As you do this, focus on the open feeling in your chest and do not allow your shoulders to move away from the wall. If you sense any tension in your lower back while doing this exercise, stand quietly and realign your body, relaxing both the hips and the shoulders, until the tension is released.

LIFTING THE RIB CAGE AND OPENING THE CHEST

Releasing the tension in your back vertebrae is an important step toward lifting the rib cage and opening the chest. Utilize the analogy of a string pulling up through the top of your head to stretch the back vertebrae upward, while at the same time keeping your shoulders relaxed and low. Breathe deeply and consciously expand your rib cage as you feel your shoulders widen and move outward and back. When you release your breath, keep your rib cage lifted and extended. As you breathe normally, sustain this lifted and open position of your chest.

For practice, deflate your chest and let it collapse into the incorrect position. Then practice lifting, inflating, and expanding the rib cage and the chest properly again. You need to be able to return to this expanded rib cage posture each time you conduct. Here are other ideas that may help you.

> **Lifting the Rib Cage and Opening the Chest**
>
> • Hands Behind Your Head
>
> • Chicken Wings
>
> • Towel Pull
>
> • Arm Lifts
>
> • Windshield Wipers
>
> **Video 1.4** ▶

Hands Behind Your Head

Lift your arms and lock your fingers behind the top of your head. As you do this, feel how the rib cage naturally lifts up. Now, bend to the side, pointing your left elbow at the floor, then bend to the other side, pointing your right elbow at the floor. Feel the stretch on each side of your body just below the rib cage.

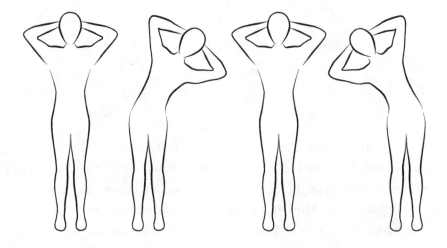

Return to the center position and bend both elbows forward and then back. This will create a stretching and contraction in the upper chest. End with your elbows out to the sides and then release your hands and slowly lower your arms, keeping your rib cage lifted.

Chicken Wings

Lift up your elbows to each side and place your thumbs lightly in your armpits as though you are making "chicken wings." Flap these wings up and down, relaxing your shoulders and consciously widening your chest. You can also imagine that your elbows are resting on two imaginary, shoulder-height walls on either side of you. As your elbows rest on these walls, relax your shoulders, but keep your rib cage up and expanded. Lower your chin and tune into how your body feels in this position.

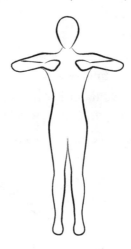

Towel Pull

Imagine that you have a towel on a table in front of you, rolled up like a long sausage. Grab each end, keeping your hands about two feet apart, and pull it until it is tight. Now raise this towel up above your head, still stretching it tightly. Move it behind your head and bring it down to rest behind your neck. As you do this, do you feel your chest expanding and opening? Lift the towel above your head again, then, bring it back down to rest even lower behind your neck on your shoulders. Do this a few times and you will notice your chest opening up even more.

Arm Lifts

While standing with your weight equally balanced and your arms by your sides, lift both arms out to your sides even with your shoulders. Did you feel the rib cage lift up along with your arms? Lower your arms back down to your sides and lift them up again. While holding your arms out, breathe in to expand your rib cage outward, keeping your shoulders relaxed and down. Feel how this expansion occurs also across your back. Repeat the exercise a few times, lowering your arms and lifting them up again.

Windshield Wipers

With your arms lifted and extended to each side, bend each arm at the elbow and turn your forearms and hands downward keeping them totally relaxed. From this position, swing your forearms and hands inward and outward like upside-down windshield wipers. While doing this, feel the open space underneath in your armpits and enjoy the floppy relaxation of your forearm and hands.

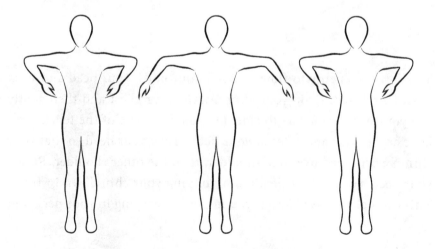

THE HEAD

When you are conducting, your body should
be grounded but your head should always feel
light and lifted. The following exercises will
ensure that energy will easily flow from your
rooted lower body, through the upper torso,
and out the top of your head.

> **The Head**
>
> • Puppet String
> • Head Rolls
> • Chin Placement
> • Book on the Head
>
> **Video 1.5** ▶

Puppet String

Imagine the puppet string coming out of the top of your head. As you
are standing, feel it lift your body as it pulls your head and neck upward. Reach up and tickle the top of your head where the imaginary
string is attached. Can you feel a sense of energy? Grab some of your
hair and pull upward and allow the chin to move downward slightly,
toward your chest. Be aware of the position of your neck as it length-
ens upward releasing the stress in your back. The chest will open up
and the vertebrae in the back will naturally extend. Breathe deeply
and try to feel a tingling in the top of your head where the string is
pulling upward. It is important to be able to connect to this tingling
feeling.

Head Rolls

To allow the energy to flow through your body, your head and neck
must be relaxed. Drop your chin toward your chest and then gently
roll your head from side to side. Do you feel some of the tension release at the back and sides of your neck? Turn your head so that your
chin is positioned over one shoulder, then the other shoulder. Rotate
your head slowly like a pendulum, dipping your chin down in front.
This can help release tension you might be carrying in your neck and
head.

Chin Placement

The placement of the chin is very important in conducting and it can easily block the flow of energy you need to send to your players. Pull your chin down so that it is almost touching your chest. Feel it stretch and lengthen the muscles and vertebrae at the back of your neck. Now tilt your chin up about two inches. Memorize this position. Your chin should always feel like it is slightly pulled back and down. Stand quietly in this position, then repeat this chin roll a few times.

Book on the Head

Return your head to its regular position and carefully place a hardcover book on your head. Choose one that is not too heavy but sturdy enough to stay in place. Slowly walk around the room, balancing the book on your head. You should be able to walk without the book falling off. Keep your body relaxed. Practice walking with the book on your head until it feels very comfortable. From this position, try conducting some basic beat patterns. Make sure that your arm movements do not cause the book to fall off your head. This exercise is excellent for balance, and for head placement.

THE SHOULDERS

As we work our way through the different parts of the body, it is important that the shoulders are always lowered and relaxed. Many people, especially conductors, carry substantial tension in their shoulders. This is something to avoid. If you are currently holding tension in your shoulders, you need to find ways to relieve that stress, both for the success of your conducting, and for your general health. Here are exercises to help relax your shoulders and to release tension in your arms.

The Shoulders

- Arm Circles
- Shoulder Lifts
- Shoulder and Arm Releases
- Go-Away Motion
- Falling Arms

Video 1.6

Arm Circles

From your standing position, lift your arms so that they are straight out from your body on either side. Now move your arms in very small circles backward. Concentrate on how your arms connect to your shoulders. As you roll your arms in a backward motion, you can feel the arms rotate in the shoulder socket. The muscles across your back will flex and relax as you rotate your arms in these small circles. Notice, how this motion widens and opens the front of your rib cage, releasing the muscles around your shoulders.

Shoulder Lifts

To further release the tension in your shoulders, let both arms hang down loosely at your sides, then lift one of your shoulders up as if you are going to try to touch it to your ear. Hold that position for a moment, then release the shoulder and let it drop down with your arm as a dead weight. Wiggle the arm slightly and feel the heavy weight of the arm pulling down on the shoulder. Lift and release the shoulder again, this time focusing on sending the tension held in the shoulder down the relaxed arm and into the floor. Do this shoulder-lifting exercise with each shoulder until they both feel relaxed.

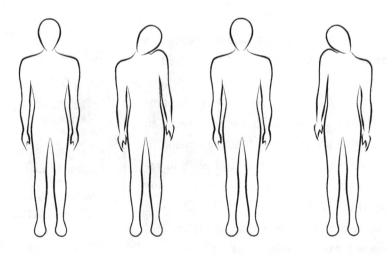

Nuzzle the Kitten

A variation of this exercise is to pretend that you have a small kitten sitting on your shoulder. Slowly raise your shoulder so you can nuzzle the kitten with your cheek. Lower your shoulder as if you are still balancing the kitten and repeat these motions with the same shoulder a few times. Switch to the other shoulder and continue the exercise an equal number of times. Now try lifting both shoulders together; two kittens, one on each shoulder. When finished, stand with your arms relaxed by your sides and feel how your shoulders have released their tension.

Shoulder and Arm Releases

Once your shoulders are more relaxed, allow your arms to hang down at your sides and focus on just one arm. Feel the weight of that arm. Jiggle your arm slightly back and forth and imagine that a heavy rock is on a string attached to your fingertips. Feel the weight of the rock pulling down on the first finger as you gently shake the arm and hand, then the second, third, and fourth fingers. Feel the rock weighing down the entire hand and arm. As you do this, you will experience the shoulder releasing even more and you might find yourself leaning slightly in that direction. Practice this exercise with each arm separately. When you finish each arm, look in a mirror. You will notice that your shoulder is lower and your arm is much more extended on that side of your body than when you started.

Go-Away Motion

For additional release of tension, you can lift each arm and make a motion to the side like you are telling someone to "go away." After this motion, let your arm flop loosely to your side. Practice this exercise five or six times with each arm.

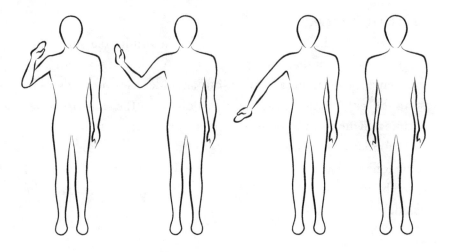

Falling Arms

Now, lift both arms up and hold them straight out to your sides, then release your shoulders and let your arms fall limply to the sides of your body. Repeat this until the arms and shoulders feel completely relaxed.

THE ARMS

The position of the arms for conducting is very important. If they are held wrong, you may experience muscle tension and stress, or you may look awkward and angular. As you raise your arms to conduct, make sure that your back feels open and extended across the shoulder blades and that you have a slightly lifted feeling under your elbows. If you touch your fingers together with your palms up in front of your belly button, the arms can create a type of circle from your shoulders.

The Arms

- Circular Placement
- Elbow Space
- Accordion Push and Pull
- Wipe the Table
- Polish the Table

Video 1.7

Circular Placement

Once you are comfortable with this circular placement of your arms, you can move your arms and hands out about 10 to 12 inches from your body. This is a good, basic conducting position. As you hold your arms there, tune into the current of energy that flows from your abdomen to your hands.

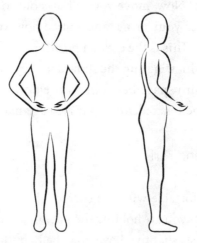

Now, rotate the hands so that the palms are facing the floor and separate them so there is about a foot of space between them. Hold that position as if your hands are resting gently on a piano keyboard in front of you. Keep a rounded feeling in your arms and make sure that your shoulders are expanded outward and not holding any tension.

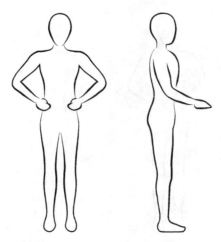

Elbow Space

Keeping your arms slightly away from your body as you conduct is important to inspire an open, released sound. With your hands resting on the keys of your imaginary piano, experiment with squeezing your elbows in to touch the sides of your body. Do you feel how the energy shifts and tightens? Now, move your elbows out to the sides again, creating a space under your arms, and notice how your chest opens and shoulders broaden. This is the correct position. Try moving your elbows back and forth again, wiggling the shoulders as you do this. Identify the correct position with space between your elbows and your sides. Your shoulders should be relaxed, and your rib cage naturally expanded.

Accordion Push and Pull

After you are comfortable with the correct placement of your arms and elbows, pretend that you are holding the sides of a small accordion in front of you at your waist, slightly above your belly button. As you pull your hands further apart to allow airflow into the accordion, feel the resistance of the bellows between your hands. Then slowly squeeze the accordion back together, still feeling the resistance of the air. Repeat this a few times. The arms and shoulders follow the motion of the hands. You should feel resistance between your hands, but never tension in your arms.

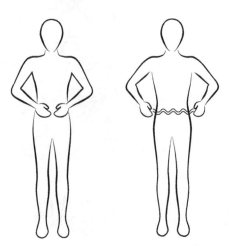

Practice pushing and pulling the bellows of your imaginary accordion as you breathe in and expand your hands and arms for four counts, and then breathe out for four counts as your hands and arms contract and meet in front of your body. Gradually extend the number of counts for each breath. Your hands should never extend more than two feet from each other. Be sure to move them slowly and evenly throughout the exercise.

Wipe the Table

To develop more control of the motions of your arms and hands, try this exercise. Reach your hand out as if you were going to place it, palm down, on a table. The table is about waist high in front of you. Now slide your hand lightly on the top of the table as though you are wiping it off. Move your hand back and forth slowly across the top of your imaginary table. Your arm and shoulder should follow the motion of the hand. Keep the motion even without any jerks or stops, and always feel that connection to the table. Now do the same motion with your other hand.

Polish the Table

Now, instead of wiping the table off, move your hand in a circular, polishing motion, on top of the imaginary table. Experiment with circles, both large and small, in clockwise and counterclockwise motions. Envision the feeling of your hand contacting the top of the table, particularly the sensation in the tips of your fingers. Practice these same motions with your other hand. Depending on whether you are right- or left-handed, one hand might perform these motions more easily and smoothly than the other. Spend extra time practicing with your weaker hand to build muscle memory and to develop both hands to the same level.

THE WRIST AND FINGERS

Conductors need to develop an independence
of the wrist and fingers to perform certain
conducting techniques. These smaller muscles need to be trained and exercised so that
you do not risk injury to them by repetitive
movements. The first step is to isolate some
of the motions you will utilize and to repeat
these motions to build muscle memory until
they feel natural and can be done without
stress.

**The Wrist
and Fingers**

- The Wrist
- Coin on Hand
- Wrist Flicks
- Wrist and Finger Taps
- Wrist Circles
- Finger Drumming
- Finger Contractions

Video 1.8

The Wrist

When you move your wrist as a conductor, you should never "break"
or "flop" the wrist. When we refer to the wrist, we are really talking
about the movement of the hand, not the actual joint where the hand
attaches to the forearm. Your actual wrist joint should always stay
level with your forearm and your hand and fingers should never be
lower than your wrist joint. When conducting, your hand will move
upward from that joint and then back down to being level with the
wrist joint.

Figuring out how to control the motion of the wrist is a stumbling
block for many conductors. You will not want your conducting gesture
to appear blocked or stiff because of locking your wrist; and you want to
avoid conducting with a wrist motion that is loose and floppy. Finding the
right balance of wrist motion and developing the muscles of the wrist to
move in the correct manner will take time and practice.

Coin on the Hand

To develop hand control and to prevent your wrist from being too flexible, or floppy, try balancing a coin on the top of your hand while you
conduct. Keep your hand even with your forearm by not bending it at the
wrist joint. Move the hand back and forth evenly in front of you at the
height of your waist and make sure you do not let the coin fall off. Try the
same thing with the other hand.

Wrist Flicks

The opposite of the "coin on hand" technique is the "wrist flicks." Imagine
that your forearm and hand are resting on a table. With your first finger
and thumb lightly touching, bend your hand up from the wrist and
quickly flick it in the air as if you are trying to shake a droplet of water off
your first finger. Flick downward and allow the hand to rebound back up.
As you do this, you should not actually touch the table with your fingers.
Now try the same motion in the air. As you flick, your hand should never
move below your forearm. The control of this gesture requires the development of specific muscles in your arm. Practice this exercise many times
with each hand to strengthen these muscles.

Wrist and Finger Taps

To develop control of the movement of your wrist, place your hand on
a table and lift your hand and fingers upward and off the table by bending upward at the wrist. While doing this, make sure that your forearm
remains solidly on the table. Now, move the hand back toward the table
and tap on the table with your fingertips, keeping your fingers slightly
curled. As you do this, you will feel muscles stretching in your forearm
and underneath your arm. Keep tapping up and down in an even rhythm.
You might want to practice this with a metronome and vary the speed of
the beat. Once you have mastered this on a real table, try the same motion

in the air. If your hand becomes tired, switch and continue with the other hand until the muscles of both hands and arms have developed.

Wrist Circles

Your wrist can also move in a sideways, circular fashion. Lay your arm on a real table and touch your first finger and thumb together. Move your hand and wrist as if you were drawing a circle with a small pencil held between your thumb and first finger. Make the circles in a clockwise motion. Feel the muscles flexing in your forearm.

Lift your hand and arm off the table and try the same motion in the air. Make sure that you control this circular motion of the wrist so that it does not become too large. After you have thoroughly exercised one hand, change to the other hand and complete the exercise again. You will find this much harder to do with your non-dominant hand. Work both hands until this gesture becomes comfortable and relaxed.

Finger Drumming

Place your forearm and wrist on a table with a pocket of air under the palm of your hand and your fingertips lightly touching the table. Now, one at a time, isolate each finger and move it up and down, tapping softly on the table. The first two fingers are the most important to develop and in some ways the easiest to manipulate, but also spend time strengthening the muscles connected to the other fingers. You will feel the individual muscles flexing in your arm as you isolate the use of each finger. You can try this same exercise in the air once you have mastered it on the table. Make sure you keep your arm and hand still as you move each finger up and down.

Finger Contractions

Now we will work on isolating finger motions at the joints. Place your hand flat on a table, with the fingers relaxed and slightly separated. Bend your fingers at the first and second joints and pull the tips of your fingers in toward the palm of your hand. To do this, you will have to lift your hand up slightly off the table. Hold this position for a few seconds, then, extend your fingers out flat again to rest on the table. Repeat this motion to develop the independence of these muscles. You can also practice this in the air.

Another variation of this can be done as follows. While you are keeping your palm level with the floor, move your fingers and thumb so that they are hanging straight downward from the top of your hand. The fingers can touch each other slightly. Contract the fingers upward so that the finger knuckles are bent all the way, keeping the first joint flat and even with the top of the hand. Extend the fingers back down again and repeat this exercise with each hand.

THE FACE AND EYES

For you to communicate with your musicians, your face needs to be relaxed, open, and inviting when you conduct. Your face should reflect the emotion of the music without becoming convoluted, or insincere. You will always want to encourage the musicians to play their best for you. Excess tension in your facial muscles will work against you and may

The Face and Eyes

- Face Scrunches
- Jaw Drop
- Eye Blinks

Video 1.9

confuse your players. Here are some ways to release tension from your face and eyes.

Face Scrunches

From your normal facial position, suddenly scrunch and tighten up all the muscles of your face. Hold this position for about five seconds. Then release and let your face relax. Feel the tension release from the muscles in your face. Breathe deeply, and repeat this exercise a few times.

Jaw Drop

Many people carry stress in their mouth and jaw. To release this tension, try dropping your jaw downward and gently massage the joint on both sides of your face. Move your lower jaw slightly to the right and to the left, all the while dropping it downward and relaxing the muscles. You should feel an extension and release of the muscles around your eyes at the same time that the jaw releases.

Placement of Tongue

As you bring your jaw up so that your mouth is gently closed, pay careful attention to the placement of your tongue in your mouth. Ideally, the tip of your tongue should rest gently against the back of your top front teeth. This position of the tongue helps to keep the muscles of your face relaxed.

Mouth and Lips

Some conductors study a score while they are singing or mouthing the music. This type of practice can result in the bad habit of moving your mouth constantly to the music during rehearsals and concerts. If you are experiencing this problem, try practicing while holding a pencil lightly between your lips, or experiment with sucking on a piece of hard candy while you are studying. This keeps the lips lightly apart in a relaxed fashion and will restrict the motion of your mouth and lips until you have retrained them not to move while you conduct.

Eye Blinks

Many of us feel tension and stress in the muscles of our head, above and behind our eyes. Eye blinks can be very effective for relaxing the muscles in the forehead. Close your eyes tightly and hold that position for a few seconds before releasing. Do this a few times. Try this the next time you are experiencing stress in your eyes and forehead. It should help to release some of your tension.

Smiling Eyes

As an extension of the eye blinks, try smiling and raising your cheek muscles right below the eyes so that your eyes feel a little squinty but are still open. This gesture softens the eyes and helps you to avoid the "bug-eye" look that conductors sometimes develop. As you practice this, make sure that your eyebrows are down and not strained upward. Experiment with raising and lowering these cheek muscles until this lifted facial position is second nature to you.

Field of Vision

The manner in which you look at the musicians is very important. As you conduct your group, you want them to believe you are looking at everyone at the same time. To do this, practice focusing your eyes straight ahead and then widen your peripheral vision, first to one side, then to the other. As you practice this, keep your face pointed forward; do not move it to either side. From your fixed point, try to see 180 degrees around you. As you look out over the ensemble, your eyes should not be focused on the individual performers; rather, you should encompass the entire group. Choose a point on the wall about five feet up from the floor. Scan with your eyes at that height, back and forth across the room without moving your head. Make sure that you are able to include everyone in your gaze. When possible, you should direct your attention to the back row, or the last stands. These musicians will have the hardest time seeing and connecting to your energy. If you focus on those farthest away, you will also be able to include everyone in front of them in your field of vision.

Now, while still focusing toward the back stands, practice turning your head slightly side to side to look at your imaginary ensemble more directly. This type of eye contact will be utilized for cues and for solo sections that require more individual attention from the conductor. Be comfortable turning your head to either side, and then experiment with turning both your head and your shoulders together to either side as you scan the area. Meanwhile, your feet, legs, and hips should stay grounded in your standard conducting position with the weight balanced on both legs.

If you are working with a chorus or an ensemble that stands on risers, you may be tempted to tilt your head up slightly to look at the full group because of the height of the risers. Be careful that you do not create stress by having your chin and neck in this upward position. It is better to keep your head level with your chin down and to look up at the ensemble with just your eyes than to put your head in a position that creates tension. Any tension in your body will *always* be reflected in the sound of the performers.

Eye Contact

Utilizing eye contact with your ensemble is very important for the quality of the performance and for developing rapport with those in your group. Make sure that you know your music well enough that you can keep your head out of the score. If possible, try to memorize large sections of the music so that you better connect to the musicians. Practice turning pages without looking down, or try putting tabs on your score so that you can turn a group of pages all at once. This way, you can have the music open to the harder sections, and you can turn from one section to another with ease.

OVERALL PRESENCE

As you can tell from the previous sections, it is very important that all of your body stress and tension be released before you put yourself in the position of conducting a musical ensemble. If your body is free from tension, you can tune into your core energy and communicate this energy more clearly to the group.

Practice sitting or standing quietly with your back straight and your shoulders back and relaxed. Focus on breathing deeply in and out. Now imagine yourself surrounded by a circle of intense energy. Feel it crackling, sizzling, and vibrating. At first you might only be able to sense this energy in an area a foot or two around you. With practice, however, you can widen and enlarge this circle. You want this energy field to be large enough to encompass your entire ensemble. Ideally, you also need to create it large enough to expand to the audience behind you when you conduct. If you can create the right energy environment, the connection you have with the ensemble and the audience will be extraordinary.

Some people associate this energy with a white light that enters your body through the top of your head, creating that tingling feeling that we talked about earlier. Others link it to a warm, empowering feeling that extends outward. To achieve this, you need a total relaxation of the body, along with an acute awareness in the mind.

Relaxed and Centered

So often, as conductors, our heads are so full of the technicalities of the score that we miss the importance of being relaxed and centered. We must be able to lift ourselves out of the "micro" and see everything from a much more global focal point. We must know the piece so well that we do not ever have to think about it. Instead, we are simply *in the music*. We *are the music*, and the music is flowing freely through us into that energy field that connects us to both the musicians and the listeners.

This energy cannot flow if there is tension in our bodies or stress in our minds. Therefore, it is important to spend time each day doing the exercises listed in this chapter to release and prevent tension, and to become more in touch with our personal energy. The next chapter explores how you can communicate energy through the direction, size, weight, and speed of your gestures.

NOTE

Many of the exercise examples in this chapter were derived from the work of Joseph Gifford who incorporated concepts of Alexander, Trager, Feldenkrais, Yoga, and Pilates technique.

Motions and Gestures

As a conductor, you must communicate all of your musical concepts to your players through gestures. Limiting yourself to just standard conducting diagrams and patterns would greatly diminish your ability to create exciting musical performances. Therefore, you need a wealth of gestures to draw on, and the knowledge to understand which gesture is most appropriate to convey the type of sound or musical idea you want to evoke.

Conducting gestures can be divided into basic categories. Each gesture has *direction, size, weight,* and *speed.* These motions vary from one another in physical action and involve different types of muscular movements. Your muscles must be isolated, individually trained, and strengthened so that each gesture becomes natural. This training is important so that you do not damage or put stress on your muscles by utilizing counterproductive movements carrying tension. Many conductors have ruined their careers because of back or shoulder problems, or tendonitis in the wrist or fingers.

DIRECTION

The motions that you will utilize as a conductor can be grouped according to the direction in which the hand or arm moves in front of your body. Each motion contains an impact point, for starting or clarifying the sound, and a release point.

Direction
- Vertical Motion
- Horizontal Motion
- Outward and Inward Motions
- Arcs
- Circles

Video 2.1

Vertical Motion

When we are conducting, we create motions on the vertical plane that either go downward or upward in front of our body. This motion is used for the downbeat and the upbeat. This vertical motion is the easiest to perform and the best starting point for becoming comfortable with your gestures.

Horizontal Motion

On the horizontal plane, the gestures move from side to side. Conducting patterns that use horizontal motions move across the body. This motion is similar to wiping off a tabletop. Horizontal conducting motions tend to be on a flat plane in front of you. Broad horizontal gestures help to clarify the differences between the downbeat and the other beats in the pattern.

Outward and Inward Motions

Conductors also utilize motions in which the hands move outward from their body toward the musicians, creating an expansive feeling. The opposite motion, which is effective for more intimate passages, involves bringing the hands and arms closer to their bodies.

Circular Motions

ARCS

Different types of circular motions, or arcs, can be used to connect beats together. You can utilize both domed arcs and bowl arcs to communicate to your ensemble.

Dome Arc   Bowl Arc

When placed at an angle, these arcs are similar to outlining the edges of a children's Christmas tree. This gesture is often used for showing subdivisions within vertical beats. Depending upon the speed and placement, the impact of each beat can happen at the end of the arc gesture, or more frequently, in the middle of the arc like a pendulum swinging.

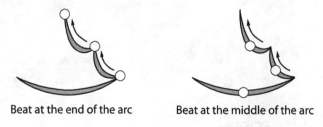

Beat at the end of the arc   Beat at the middle of the arc

CIRCLES

Circular and oval motions are very effective in communicating a continuous sense of musical line. The conducting circles motion is usually done clockwise. Notice that the impact is not at the bottom of the circle, as you might expect, but slightly delayed with the impact of the beat occurring where the number seven would be on a clock.

SIZE

The size of the conducting beat is important. Size is controlled by the various muscles and joints utilized for each gestures. When you are conducting a small beat pattern, you may be using only your fingers. As you gradually beat larger, the gesture changes, and you will begin to conduct with the hand, bending it up slightly from the joint where your hand joins your wrist. For a medium-size beat, you will shift the motion from the hand to the forearm, bending your arm at the elbow. When you conduct with the forearm, the wrist should be still and not bent. For the largest-size beat, you will use your entire arm from the shoulder joint. Your forearm and wrist will move with the entire arm, not separately.

Practice isolating these different parts of your arm so that you can conduct beat patterns of different sizes. Remember that the connection to the ensemble always begins from the tip of the baton, or the tip of the fingers, if you are not using a baton. The wrist, forearm, or full arm, control the specific motion of the baton's tip. (See Video 2.2. ▶)

Very small beat	fingers
Small beat	hand/wrist
Medium beat	forearm
Large beat	full arm/shoulder

WEIGHT AND RESISTANCE

As you conduct, each of your gestures should convey a feeling of weight, or imaginary resistance. The easiest way to think about this is to remember the way your arms feel when you move them in a swimming pool. They cannot move as fast in water as they move in the air. The weight of the water presses against your arms and creates resistance. You need to be able to create the same sense of resistance, or weight, as you conduct in the air.

The following are some examples of how to communicate weight and resistance. Notice that weight tends to be related to an upward motion, as if you are picking something up, while resistance tends to be related to a side-to-side, or a forward-backward motion, where you are pushing or pulling against something. Experiment with these different motions and resistance levels. (See Video 2.3. ▶))

Picking up a feather	light weight
Picking up a can of food	medium weight
Picking up a heavy rock	heavy weight
Pulling taffy	light resistance
Moving your hand in water	medium resistance
Pushing against a brick wall	heavy resistance

SPEED

The speed of a gesture is also a factor in conducting. We have beats that range from *very slow, slow, medium, fast,* and *very fast,* depending upon the tempo of the piece. When isolating the concept of speed, it is useful to set a metronome on a very slow tempo and to beat time to it while gradually increasing the tempo. As you do this, make sure that the size of the beat stays exactly the same. If the size is the same, yet the tempo is faster, the speed of each beat must increase. In this manner, you can experience the increase of speed on the beat. You may find it harder to sustain the even motion of a slow beat compared to conducting quickly. Work on strengthening the muscles that control the slow beats so you can perform these gestures smoothly without shaking or using extraneous motions.

ENERGY

In addition to understanding the direction, size, weight, and speed of the beat, we must also take into account the *energy* level of each gesture, and the specific *impact*, or moment of *contact* and *release*. These create the character and clarity of each beat. There are moments when a clear, accented beat is vitally important, and there are moments when a fluid, connected beat is essential. Being able to switch instantaneously between the two is necessary to develop an effective conducting technique.

Energy defines the way a gesture communicates to a group of musicians. Each motion contains an inherent energy built into it. When you pick something up, there is *energy away* from your contact point as you lift it up. When you hit a ball with a bat, there is *energy toward* the contact point. Understanding the difference between energy toward the beat and energy away from the beat can help you communicate better as a conductor. The type of energy used will often define the type of impact and release for that specific gesture. Each gesture will create a unique sound or musical attack from the ensemble.

Active Energy

Any energy that is moving either toward something or away from something is an *active energy*. This type of energy almost feels alive in our hands. If you rub your hands together and then hold them apart with the palms facing each other, the tingling you feel between them is a sense of energy. You want to create that same energy connection between each of your conducting motions.

You can transfer this energy from one beat to the other with a slight release of the energy after each impact point. Energy is communicated through a combination of showing weight, resistance, and speed.

When you conduct slow, sustained music, there will be *continuous energy* between beats, with no release of this energy. This is difficult to show because you must communicate the actual beat without stopping the motion, or the energy. This type of energy is used for sustained whole notes or for slow legato passages.

Some motions are naturally preceded by a breath or preparatory gesture (*prep*). A prep beat contains an active energy and it is one of the most important gestures to master in conducting. Every time you start your ensemble, you will need to show a preparatory beat. This prep beat will always have energy moving toward the beat, and it is an essential gesture for starting the ensemble together. The breath that accompanies the preparatory beat must be given in exactly the same tempo that you want the ensemble to play. Practicing gestures that have a natural preparatory movement will help you to understand how basic this motion is and how the preparatory gesture leads directly into the contact point of the starting beat.

Passive Energy

Conducting also uses gestures that have no real active energy but instead are *passive* in nature. Passive energy gestures are used when nothing is happening in the music. This gesture is not limp or motionless; rather, the motions are clear but they are shown without any feeling of weight or resistance. An example might be the manner in which you place your hand on a table. There is really no energy in the motion; you just put your hand down. This type of gesture is used to show a *dead beat*, or a *silent beat*.

Passive energy gestures can be fast or slow, depending upon the music, but this gesture must never convey any emotion or character. To do so, would confuse the musicians in front of you and might make them enter at the wrong time. Because we are so used to constantly sending active energy out to our ensemble, it is difficult to master these dead, passive energy gestures. Being able to clearly conduct passive beats is critically important for conducting rests, fermatas, and recitatives.

Group Energy

Besides active and passive energy gestures, an overall *group energy* is constantly being exchanged between you and the people around you. Think again of the tingling on the top of your head from earlier in the book and practice transferring this energy to the performing group in front of you. Remaining calm and breathing deeply while conducting will help you to increase this energy level. In a concert situation, you must also send this energy to the audience behind you.

IMPACT AND RELEASE

Preparatory Beats

The *preparatory beat* is a motion that occurs before the gesture that shows the impact. This motion is necessary to prepare for the desired type of musical attack and to communicate the volume and quality of the sound that you want. It is similar to the motion of pulling your arm back with a tennis racket before you swing to strike the ball. Many of our motions in everyday life are preceded by some sort of preparatory gesture. To bounce a ball, you first lift up your hand. Before you can sing,

> **Impact and Release**
>
> • Preparatory Beats
> • The Ictus
> • The Rebound
> • Smooth Impact
> • Dead Beats
> • Basic Conducting Beat Patterns
>
> **Video 2.4**

you must take a breath. Understanding how the preparatory gesture sets the quality, articulation, and speed of the music is critical to becoming a good conductor.

The Ictus

The exact point of impact of the beat is called the *ictus.* The ictus is a sharp motion that is produced by either the fingers or the hand/wrist motion. You can experience the feeling of connecting to the ictus more clearly if you imagine that you have a drop of water on the tip of the baton, and then you flick your hand to shake the water off. The flick creates the ictus, or the impact point of the beat at the tip of the baton.

The ictus beat is used for staccato and marcato passages, and for passages with intricate rhythms. Sometime, this ictus is a sharp tap for a fast, loud, and accented entrance. Other times, it is a soft pressing gesture without a "click" or sharp motion. Understanding that there are different types of ictus can give you much more variety and control of the sound from your ensemble.

The Rebound

After the ictus, there is movement away for the impact point that releases the sound. We refer to this as the *rebound*. The concept is similar to bouncing on a trampoline; you push down and impact the trampoline, and then it bounces you up in the air. Another example would be the bounce of a basketball; the ball hits the floor and then bounces up. In general, the rebound stroke should not come up as high as the original beat. The exception to this would be when you are beating patterns of one beat to the bar, when the rebound would have to return to the original starting point.

Smooth Impact

For legato sections, you should not use a beat with a sharp ictus. Instead, you would utilize a motion with a smooth impact, similar to the contact of a ball with a tennis racket as you swing it, or the path of a pendulum. This type of motion does not stop. You are aware of the moment of impact, but the overall motion moves smoothly through the beat and continues. This type of gesture includes a *follow-through* motion instead of a rebound; the hand, forearm, or arm continues to move in the same trajectory after passing through the point of the beat. The energy moves forward to the actual beat point, and then is released after the imaginary impact.

Dead Beats

We also have gestures that are called *dead* or *stopped* beats. This type of motion does not have impact, rebound, or follow-through. The hand simply moves to the point of the beat without energy, stops, and then after a moment moves to the next beat and stops again. This is a very important technique to master for conducting musical sections of rests or recitative.

Basic Conducting Beat Patterns

Over time, certain patterns of moving the hand have been established to communicate to the ensemble the specific beats within each measure. Each ensemble member looks at the position of your hand in front of your body to determine where you are in the measure. In this manner, the ensemble is able to play together.

In Chapter 3, we will delve more deeply into the various types of conducting beat patterns, but to get you started, here are some basic diagrams for conducting meters of 1, 2, 3, and 4.

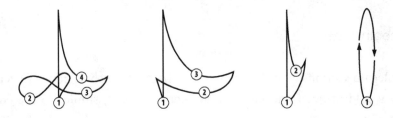

GESTURES YOU ALREADY KNOW

Now that we have covered the basic parameters of conducting motions, let us see if we can understand, isolate, and practice a variety of gestures to train our muscle memory and allow us to better understand the function and relationship of the movements of our fingers, hand, wrist, forearm, elbow, full arm, and shoulder. To do this, we will utilize motions and gestures that you know well and have performed before at some point in your life.

Each set of examples will focus on a specific movement, beginning with the smallest way to perform the gesture, then progressing to the largest size of the gesture. In this way, you will be able to separate and develop your use of finger flexibility, hand/wrist motion, forearm movement, and full arm/shoulder motion.

At the same time, each example will also force you to gradually increase your understanding of weight and resistance. Showing weight and resistance through your gestures is essential to communicating tone quality and musical texture to your musicians. You will want to practice until you are able to communicate subtle differences of weight and resistance clearly and with ease.

We start by grouping the gestures according to their basic direction: downward and upward, side to side, and outward and inward. As you practice these motions, even if you are left-handed, use your right hand, just as you would if you were conducting an ensemble. Repeat each gesture until your hand performs the motion smoothly without tension. Focus your attention on the way your muscles are moving and reacting and do not just mindlessly mime the exercises. You want to use the repetition of these gestures as a means of training the muscles of your arm and hand, and also sharpening your mind so that the gesture becomes ingrained.

THE DOWNWARD GESTURE

The downward gesture is a great starting point for training your muscles and it is the easiest to understand. We use the downward gesture for all types of everyday tasks. Sometime the motion has weight connected to it, as when you are pulling down a window shade. At other times, the weight might only be the actual weight of your hand or arm. Some of your downward gestures will naturally stop at their point of contact, like placing a hand on a table. Other downward gestures will connect for an instant to the contact point, and then naturally release that contact, like lifting your hand from a hot stove.

Experiment with the following downward gestures. They are grouped so that you will be able to separate the important components of size, weight, contact, and release. Practice these motions until you understand the subtle muscle differences among them. Do these first in the order they are written, and then alternate between them. Focus on the different types of resistance, the contact point, and the various releases of energy that are involved with these downward strokes. (See Video 2.5. ▶)

MOTION DOWNWARD—CONTACT—THEN RELEASE

Typing on a computer	fingers
Tapping someone on the shoulder	hand/wrist
Bouncing a basketball	forearm
Bouncing a basketball very high	full arm

Motion downward—contact—then stop

Turning off a light switch	fingers
Playing and holding a note on a piano	hand/wrist
Placing your hand on a baby's head	forearm
Drawing a line downward on a chalkboard	full arm

Motion downward with resistance—contact—then stop

Sliding a dimmer switch down	fingers
Closing a Jack-in-the-Box toy	hand/wrist
Pulling down a window shade	forearm
Painting the fence with a downward stroke	full arm

THE UPWARD GESTURE

The upward gesture is, of course, a motion that primarily goes up. Sometimes, this gesture is preceded by a small, passive downward gesture to get you in the right position for the upward stroke, but the focus remains on the upward gesture. With this motion, the energy moves upward, and the energy occurs after, and away from, the actual contact point. The upward gesture is often associated with the thought of picking something up. This lifting upward is connected to different levels of weight and energy. Depending upon what you are picking up, the weight and resistance involved with upward gestures of this type will vary greatly. (See Video 2.6. ▶)

Contact—weight—motion upward—stop

Picking crumbs off the table	fingers
Picking up a pea	hand/wrist
Lifting your coffee cup	forearm
Picking up a heavy rock with one hand	full arm

Experimenting with Weight

It is essential for you to develop the ability to convincingly convey a sense of a variety of weights through similar gestures. Often, the gesture will remain the same size with the same basic characteristics, but the conveyed sense of weight or resistance will change. Experiment with the examples below and see if you are able to show the difference between the weights of the objects listed. Strive to physically show the difference in these motions, even though you are not picking up the actual item. Tune in to your muscles and evaluate what changes you need to make to convey this sense of weight. Check yourself in a mirror to see if you are successful, or have a friend watch and guess what you are picking up. If you are having trouble, try lifting the actual objects until you become used to the real weight involved with each item, then try the gesture again with just your hand. When you have mastered these exercises, be creative and experiment with a few new ones of your own. (See Video 2.7. ▶)

One Hand

Plucking a piece of hair	fingers
Sliding a dimmer switch up	fingers
Picking up a salt shaker	hand/wrist
Picking up a can of corn	hand/wrist
Lifting up a dry towel	forearm
Lifting up a wet towel	forearm or full arm
Picking up an empty book bag	forearm
Picking up a full book bag	forearm or full arm

Two Hands

Sometimes while conducting, you may choose to use two hands together to convey a certain mood or feeling, or to achieve a larger, fuller sound. This involves showing a variety of weight and resistance in your gesture to communicate different types of sound quality. When you use two hands in this manner, your hands will mirror each other and the energy will be focused on the imaginary object or contact point between your two hands. As you practice these motions, see if you can imagine the difference in sound that each gesture would evoke.

Picking up an empty flower vase	forearms
Picking up a full flower vase	forearms
Picking up a volleyball	forearms
Picking up a bowling ball	forearms
Picking up a pile of laundry	full arms
Picking up a large, heavy rock	full arms

Lifted from Beneath

There are situations when you are not actually lifting things with your hands but rather feeling that your hands are naturally being lifted up by a force beneath them, almost without effort. This motion happens slowly and evenly. It is a useful gesture to master in order to convey natural buoyancy to the sound. Here are a few examples for you to practice with one or both hands.

- Imagine that your hands are above a heater vent and the warm air is gently pushing them up.
- Rest your hand on top of a helium balloon; feel it rise up underneath and lift your hand.
- Rest both your hands on top of an imaginary elevator and feel it lift your hands upward.

SIDEWAYS GESTURES

Gestures that move from side to side horizontally are the most frequently used in conducting. It is within these broader horizontal gestures that you are able to convey the variety of character and style that is so important in bringing a piece of music to life. To do this, you need to master moving smoothly in both directions, right to left, and left to right. You also need to perfect the ability to change direction without a jerk or hesitation in the motion, similar to how violinists change the direction of the bow arm.

When you are using horizontal gestures, you will be dealing mostly with what I call the *flat plane*, directly in front of your body. I refer to this flat plane as the *table of sound* and it becomes the point where you connect to the sound of the ensemble. The gestures you practice on this flat plane will move from side to side on top of this imaginary table.

There is also another placement for horizontal gestures called the *wall plane*. It is located in front of your body like an imaginary chalkboard. Although less common, gestures and motions can move in a side-to-side motion across this wall plane in front of your body, as if you are writing on a chalkboard.

Here are some sideways gestures to practice on the flat plane and the wall plane. Once again, focus on the individual muscles you are utilizing for each motion. Your motions should be even, and you must refine changing directions smoothly without a stop or bump. Your attention and energy must always be connected to the imaginary object in front of you. (See Video 2.8. ▶)

MOTION SIDEWAYS—HORIZONTAL FLAT PLANE

Brushing the dust off something very small	fingers
Wiping the white keys of the piano	hand/wrist
Sweeping off a table with a small brush	forearm
Running your hand along the hood of a car	full arm

MOTION SIDEWAYS—HORIZONTAL WALL PLANE

Wiggling your finger sideways	fingers
Waving goodbye	hand/wrist
Moving your hand and arm like a windshield wiper	forearm
Erasing the chalkboard	full arm

As we add weight and resistance to our horizontal motions, you should feel a difference in how you perform each gesture. Connect with the various levels of weight and resistance as you practice the exercises below. How do these gestures feel compared to the ones you did earlier?

MOTION SIDEWAYS—WITH WEIGHT/RESISTANCE—FLAT PLANE

Wiping a smudge off the table with your finger	finger
Spreading butter on bread	hand/wrist
Ironing clothes	forearm
Dragging a wet towel across a swimming pool	full arm

MOTION SIDEWAYS—WITH WEIGHT/RESISTANCE—WALL PLANE

Browsing through a sample book with your finger	fingers
Pushing open a curtain	hand/wrist
Opening a sliding cabinet door	forearm
Opening a sliding glass door	full arm

Release of Gesture

The way a gesture is released is also very important. Most of the previous examples involved the *turn-around* motion, where you are striving to smoothly connect each of the sideways gestures. There are times, however, when you will want the gesture to go in only one direction, followed by a lift, or release, of the sound. You can still move in both directions, but the overall gesture is not connected; instead, the contact is released each time, and re-engaged with the next stroke. Try these exercises in both directions—right to left, then left to right.

MOTION SIDEWAYS—RELEASE—FLAT PLANE

Petting a mouse	fingers
Petting a cat	hand/wrist
Petting a goat	forearm
Brushing a horse with long strokes	full arm

Opposite Motions

It is also important to practice sideways motions using both hands, where our hands move in opposite directions, out to both sides of our body. This gesture is used to show how long notes are held, and it requires the ability to move slowly with extended, sustained energy. The different sizes and resistances of the gesture can be correlated with the volume and intensity of sound that you want the performers to produce.

MOTION SIDEWAYS IN OPPOSITE DIRECTIONS— WITH WEIGHT/RESISTANCE—FLAT PLANE (BOTH HANDS)

Separating a sticky label from the paper	fingers
Pulling a piece of taffy	hands/wrists
Stretching a large rubber band	forearms
Having a tug of war with yourself	full arms

MOTIONS OUTWARD

An alternate conducting position is achieved by moving your arms from their regular position to a place forward and out from the body. This motion of moving *outward,* or away from your body, can create a feeling of expansiveness that communicates differently to your players.

When performing outward motions, the position of the hand and arm can either be in an *overhand* position, where the palm is turned flat toward the floor; a *sideways* position, with the palm to the side; or an *underhand* position, where the palm of your hand is facing upward.

As you experiment with turning your hand from being flat to the floor, to being sideways to the floor, and then to facing completely upward, feel the manner in which the bones of the forearm twist and change positions. The muscles of the upper arm must adjust slightly as you make this change in the placement of your hand. Focus on the different feelings of the underhand and overhand motion in the outward gesture as you work your way through these examples. (See Video 2.9. ▶)

Motion outward—overhand

Pressing on a buzzer or doorbell	fingers
Knocking on a door	hand/wrist
Pushing away your coffee cup	forearm
Hitting a punching bag	full arm

Motion outward—sideways hand

Flicking a pea	fingers
Lighting a match	hand/wrist
Dealing cards	forearm
Throwing a Frisbee	full arm

Motion outward—underhand

Balancing an object on your palm and moving your hand forward	full arm

Motion Outward with Two Hands

Occasionally, you might want to use the outward gesture with two hands. Usually this will occur with the hands in the overhand position. Here are some motions that utilize various weights and resistances to help you to become acquainted with the feel of the two-handed outward gesture.

Using a rolling pin	forearms
Pressing both hands against a wall	full arms

MOTIONS INWARD

The *inward* gesture is the opposite of the outward gesture and involves moving your hands and arms closer to your body. This can be used to communicate softer dynamics for more intimate passages. This gesture can also be performed using either an *underhand, sideways,* or *overhand* position of the palm of your hand. Feel the difference as you practice gestures that move inward toward your body. Focus on the contact point and the resistance of the object you imagine you are moving or interacting with. (See Video 2.10. ▶))

MOTION INWARD—UNDERHAND

Wiping a drop of water from underneath a shelf   fingers
Taking a piece of paper from someone   hand/wrist

MOTION INWARD—SIDEWAYS

Sliding your pile of poker chips toward you   forearm
Pulling on a large rope   full arm

MOTION INWARD—OVERHAND

Scratching the top of a table   fingers
Digging a little hole in the dirt with your hand   hand/wrist
Pulling a small drawer open   forearm
Dragging a heavy bag of rocks toward you   full arm

Inward with Two Hands

You can also use a two-handed gesture that moves inward. This, like the outward gesture, is usually done with the hands in the overhand position. It can be a more powerful gesture than the one-handed inward gesture. Using the two hands can help focus the sound of the ensemble as you bring them to you.

MOTION INWARD—BOTH HANDS TOGETHER

Sliding the dimmers down on a lighting board   fingers
Brushing the crumbs off the table into your lap   hands/wrist
Opening a dresser drawer   forearms
Rowing a boat (pulling toward you)   full arms

CIRCLES, ARCS, AND FREE MOTIONS

Other types of motions that can be used to convey conducting gestures are *circles, arcs,* and *free motions*. With each of these, the hand moves in a rounded or curved manner, as opposed to the straight lines of the inward and outward gestures. These motions can be made on either the flat plane of the table of sound, or on the wall plane in front of your body. (See Video 2.11. ▶))

Circles

The *circle* gesture tends to be continuous. There is a perceived point of impact for each beat, but the motion of the circle does not stop. Circular gestures move clockwise and require a flexibility of the muscles of the hand, wrist, and arm that is different from the muscles used in vertical and horizontal gestures. Developing these muscles is important to give you more variety and control in your conducting. Pieces that involve a one beat pulse to a measure will usually be conducted with a circular or oval motion.

CIRCULAR MOTION—WALL PLANE

Lightly rotating the hands on a clock (clockwise)	fingers
Reeling in a fishing line	hand/wrist
Reeling in a garden hose	forearm
Wiping off the chalkboard with a large circular motion	full arm

CIRCULAR MOTION—FLAT PLANE

Stirring your cup of coffee with a plastic stick	fingers
Stirring a pot on the stove	hand/wrist
Polishing the hood of your car in a circular motion	forearm
Polishing a much larger area of the hood of your car	full arm

Arcs

The *arc* gesture is very useful for communicating subtle nuances and for musical articulations and passages that involve an upward lift of the sound. Instead of moving in a straight line, the fingers or hand outline a curved arc. On the flat plane, the gesture can be shown as either a *dip arc* as though you are outlining the inside of a bowl, or a *dome arc* where you trace the top of a dome.

Dip arc	Trace with your fingers the inside curve of a large bowl. Then try tracing the curve of different-size bowls.
Dome arc	Trace your fingers over the top of a volleyball. Then trace the top of smaller-size balls.

We also have arcs that move outward (*outward arc*) and those that move inward toward our bodies (*inward arc*). When making an arc gesture, we are moving from one contact point to another, usually on the horizontal plane, but the gesture is more expressive because of the arc motion. Many of the conducting beat patterns in legato and slow passages use different types of arcs to help give more shape to the phrase.

Outward arc	Imagine pushing a door open, out and away from your body.
Inward arc	Imagine pulling a door closed toward you.

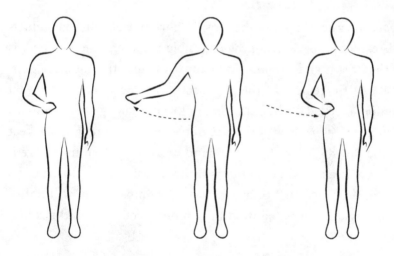

The wall plane can also be used for an arc-type motion instead of a straight line motion. Any time you are using a gesture that has part of a circle in it, you are utilizing an arc:

Arc motion *wall plane*	Outline a children's Christmas tree with your finger. Start at the top and move downward, then reverse and start at the bottom, and move upward.

Free Motion

When conducting with *free motions,* your fingers, hands, and arms do not follow any predetermined pattern of straight lines, circles, or arcs. These more random gestures are useful to practice in order to loosen muscles and to release body tension. Because of their spontaneity, gestures of this type can help make the sound more free and playful. Experiment with the free motions below and develop some exercises of your own.

Finger wiggles	fingers
Shaking your hand out	hand/wrist
Shooing a fly	forearm
Waving your arms around	full arm

PREPARATORY BEATS, CONTACT, AND RELEASE

The *preparatory beat* is one of the most important elements of conducting. It is essential for starting the ensemble together. The *prep* beat is simply the breath and motion that happens before the sound begins. This beat sets the tempo for the piece, so it must be given in the exact same tempo or speed of the beats that follow it. Many gestures contain a natural preparatory beat. In the examples below, a preparatory beat sets up the downward gesture; the hand or arm must go up before it comes down. Practice these gestures while focusing your attention on the natural prep beat that occurs before each impact. You will notice that each impact beat is followed by a spontaneous rebound gesture. (See Video 2.12. ▶)

Prep—motion downward—contact—rebound

Tapping someone softly on the shoulder	fingers
Playing with a yo-yo	hand/wrist
Bouncing a basketball	forearm or full arm

Here are some more motions that employ a preparatory beat, this time with an ictus and release. How is this prep different from the ones above?

Do you notice a slight pause at the top as you change directions? Notice the way the focus has shifted to a sharper impact, or ictus. After the impact occurs, all the energy is released quickly and you almost disconnect from the gesture.

Subtle differences in the gestures can produce completely different types of musical attacks and entrances from an ensemble. The first set of gestures in this section are best for creating a more sponge-like legato entrance with very little attack, while the following gestures will give you a precise staccato entrance and an articulation with space between the notes. All of these gestures focus the motion and energy within the downward direction.

PREP—MOTION DOWNWARD—ICTUS—RELEASE

Shaking a drop of water off your finger	fingers
Hammering a small nail	hand/wrist
Hammering a large nail	forearm
Hitting a drum medium loud	forearm
Hitting a drum loudly	full arm

In contrast, some gestures focus the energy upward. The following set of gestures utilizes a prep motion that moves toward the main contact point, followed by motion upward, away from the initial point of impact. We thus remain connected to the weight and resistance of the gesture. There is no moment of release, although the motion naturally slows near the top.

PREP—CONTACT—MOTION UPWARD—CONNECTED

Pulling out a long pin	fingers
Dipping your finger into cake batter and lifting it up	hand/wrist
Sticking your hand in mud, then lifting it up	forearm
Lifting up a large bowling ball	full arm

The following examples focus on gestures that move in an upward direction with a sharp ictus and release. Use a passive prep beat as you reach downward for the contact, and then a sharp pulling movement upward that eventually releases the energy and resistance at the top.

Prep—ictus—motion upward—release

Touching a hot stove with your finger	finger
Picking weeds	hand/wrist
Plucking a chicken	forearm
Pulling a large plant out of the ground	full arm

We also have motions involving both a preparatory gesture and an ictus that move forward and outward from our body. With these gestures, the ictus is a fast, sharp point of impact. The difference is that this motion moves forward toward our wall plane, not down toward the floor or up toward the ceiling. After the moment of impact, the hand releases quickly.

Prep—motion forward—ictus—release

Putting dabs of paint on a painting on an easel	fingers
Popping a balloon with a pin	hand/wrist
Throwing a dart	forearm
Hitting a volleyball (overhand serve)	full arm

A similar forward motion occurs with the next examples, except that instead of a sharp, jabbing ictus attack, the impact contact point happens more slowly. You will exert continuous pressure before finally releasing. When the release happens, the hand does not rebound, but rather stays nearby. This is a different type of energy and a different type of beat. It is useful for strong chords or held notes.

Prep—motion forward—impact—hold

Sticking in a thumbtack	fingers
Ringing a doorbell buzzer	hand/wrist
Hitting a punching bag	forearm or full arm
Spearing something	full arm

This last gesture can be done sideways, or in front of the body. Most important, the gesture contains a follow-through motion that passes through the point of the beat, or the point of contact. The follow-through gesture continues in the same direction as the initial motion, similar to hitting a ball with a bat or a racket, or fencing with a sword.

PREP—MOTION SIDEWAYS (OR FORWARD)—IMPACT—FOLLOW THROUGH

Hitting a ping-pong ball with the paddle	hand/wrist or forearm
Hitting a tennis ball with your racket (forehand)	full arm
Hitting a tennis ball with your racket (backhand)	full arm
Fencing with a sword	full arm

DEVELOPING THE LEFT HAND

Once you have completed all the exercises in this section with your right hand, you should start at the beginning and perform each of them with your left hand. If you are naturally right-handed, using your left hand might feel awkward and stiff. If you are left-handed, you might have experienced this problem when doing the exercises the first time with your right hand. It is important to practice all the preceding exercises with the left hand until they are natural and smooth in order to develop the hand and arm muscles that support these movements. Even though many of these gestures are motions that you do every day, you cannot expect to execute them perfectly the first time you try them with your non-dominant hand.

As you practice, do not be discouraged; it might take a long time to become skilled in performing all of these gestures. Developing muscle memory in your hands and arms is the foundation for everything you will do as a conductor. It is like a young writer learning new vocabulary words. Each new gesture, like a new word, must be learned, memorized, and mastered. In the next two chapters, we will explore ways of applying each of these gestures to achieve the best musical results.

Connecting to the Sound

Now that you have experimented with a variety of motions, it is time to apply them in a musical context. Every conducting gesture you make will produce a corollary sound and articulation from your musicians. The placement of each gesture and the lift of your breath are critical for controlling the entrance attack and the quality of the sound. The clarity of your motion and the ability to convey a consistent pulse is important for accurate ensemble playing. You must connect to your musicians in a way that enables them to play their best. Mastering your connection to the energy between you and the players is essential for communicating your concept of the music.

THE CONDUCTING STRIKE ZONE

The core of your conducting gestures are focused in an area that I call the *conducting strike zone.* This area is about one foot in front of your body, where your hand would naturally be if you extended it slightly outward, and extends from your chin down to just below your hips. The width of the strike zone is about the same as your torso, or the distance between your shoulders. In this space, you will engage and connect to the ensemble. If you move your hands out of this area, your gestures will lack focus and intensity, and the sound may become diffused. (See Video 3.1. ▶)

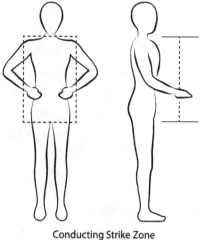

Conducting Strike Zone

Connecting to Energy

Conducting is all about connecting your energy to the energy of the musicians. Start by moving your arms up and down within the strike zone area. A feeling of energy should come out from your torso around your abdomen and flow through to your hands. Tune into this energy and this connection to your core.

> **Connecting to Energy**
>
> • Lump of Clay
> • Marshmallow
> • Water Resistance
>
> **Video 3.2**

Now place your hands together in front of you and rub them together. Then, slowly separate your hands by moving them away from each other, keeping your palms facing each other. Feel the pull of this energy between your two hands. As you move the hands farther apart, you may find it harder to keep the intensity of energy. As you extend them outside the strike zone, the energy connection with your own body may lessen. Moving out of this strike zone area can reduce your effectiveness as a conductor because of this loss of energy.

Lump of Clay

Imagine that there is a large lump of soft clay, almost a foot in diameter in the conducting strike zone in front of your stomach. Work this clay with your hands. Squeeze it and shape it. Feel its resistance. Press each of your fingers into it separately and knead it with the palms of your hands. Connect to the resistance and texture of the clay. Focus your energy and attention into this mass.

Marshmallow

Now, instead of clay, imagine that there is a very large marshmallow in front of you. Touch it with your fingers. Squeeze it gently. How does it feel different from the clay? Press and release your palms on each side of this giant marshmallow. Feel the sponginess between your fingers. Focus on connecting to this sticky, springy substance.

Water Resistance

We have all spent time in a swimming pool pulling our arms against the resistance of the water in order to swim. Imagine that you are standing in a pool of water that comes up to your shoulders. Gently push your hands through the water utilizing the conducting strike zone space. As you do this, gradually move your hands outward to both sides as if you are doing the breast stroke, and imagine the water contact on your hands and arms as you make this motion. Move your hands slowly and evenly, feeling the resistance at all times. Then reverse the gesture and move your hands back together in front of your body, pushing the water while letting it glide through your fingers. Memorize this feeling of the continuous contact and resistance of the water.

Levels of Resistance

As we conduct, we are challenged to create the illusion of a variety of resistances in the air in front of us. We use gestures that imply resistance to help shape the sound we want to draw from the musicians. The weight, or resistance, shown in the gesture communicates the type of sound desired.

What other types of resistance can you imagine? To be effective as a conductor, you must develop a sense of the different weights and energies of imaginary objects, and understand how the illusion of this weight influences the sound that the musicians will produce.

THE TABLE OF SOUND

Moving through the conductor's strike zone is an imaginary line or plane that I call the *table of sound*. All conducting gestures take place on, or slightly into, this imaginary table of sound. It is the contact point where we connect to our players and inspire the essence of the music. This table of sound lies about the height of your waist and is a flat plane across the strike zone area, similar to having an actual table in front of you.

> **The Table of Sound**
>
> • Hard-Surface Table
> • Spongy-Surface Table
> • The Transparent Table
> • The Shelf
>
> **Video 3.3**

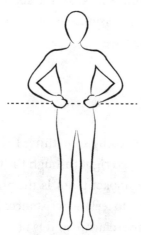

Table of Sound

This table of sound is about a foot away from your body, as an actual table might be if you were seated at it having a meal. It should feel very natural to place your hand on this table of sound. The basic impact point for your hand to touch the table should be the same for all of your gestures. It is important that the height of your imaginary table stays the same and that you do not change it for different beats.

Hard-Surface Table

When you actually tap on a real table in front of you, there is a definite feeling of resistance at the point of impact. You cannot move your hand through the table and there is no flexibility or softness. You are striking a hard, unmovable object. Practice tapping softly on your imaginary table of sound, and then tap with more force and energy. Feel the exact point of impact with your fingertips.

Spongy-Surface Table

You can also imagine a table of sound that is spongy and soft to the touch, as if you are pressing on a thick layer of cotton on the table's surface. Tap on this layer of cotton, then tap on the hard surface of the table. Experience how these gestures feel different. With the spongy-surface table you will feel the softness and slight resistance before your fingers reach the stopping point of the table's surface.

The Transparent Table

The least resistance is created by something I call the *transparent table*. With this, your hands will go right through the table, like going through the surface of water. The impact point is the point at which your hand enters the water and begins to feel the resistance. The resistance is released when the hand moves upward again and is no longer in contact with the table of sound or the imaginary surface of the water.

The Shelf

After you are comfortable with motions involving your table of sound, you can also imagine a secondary table of sound that is slightly higher, called the *shelf*. While keeping your shoulders down and relaxed, place your hands in front of you at about the same level as your heart. Practice conducting in this area with different types of weight and resistance. This shelf level can be used for conducting softer or lighter passages when you want a more transparent sound.

PLACEMENT OF THE ARM AND HAND

Many conductors have trouble establishing the proper placement of their arms and hands for conducting. Their gestures become angular, or strained and tense, which is exactly the opposite of the effect you want to convey. In order to establish a good arm position, place your right hand in front of your body as if you are going to shake hands with a colleague. Remember to keep an open space under your arm. This position should feel natural, with the arm slightly bent, not extended straight out. Now, rotate the palm of your hand toward the floor. This creates a relaxed, standard position for conducting.

When conducting with just the hand, you should always lead with the fingers. The impact of the beat will be established when the longest finger hits the imaginary table of sound in front of you. When conducting with a baton, this impact point is shifted away from the fingers to the tip of the baton. The focus of the energy must always remain at this point of impact.

Imaginary Piano

Another way to achieve the correct position of the conducting arm in relationship to your table of sound is to simply imagine that you have a piano keyboard in front of you. Now, lift up your right hand and place your finger on middle C. Play four quarter notes on middle C with this finger. Feel how your finger connects to the piano and creates the sound with its contact and release of the imaginary key. Play steady quarter notes on middle C with a forte dynamic. Then experiment with playing notes at a pianissimo dynamic. Strike the key with a sharper, faster attack, then a slow, soft attack. Play repeated notes that are longer and sustained, then experiment with a more staccato articulation. Feel the connection between your gesture and the imaginary keyboard as you imagine the sound that each motion would produce. (See Video 3.4. ▶)

SIDEWAYS MOTION

Now, imagine playing middle C, C an octave below, back to middle C, C an octave above, then return to middle C, and repeat the process. Do this with your either your first finger or middle finger striking the key. Feel the slight resistance of the key under your finger. Hear the quality of the sound with the attack and release of the note in your head. Continue alternating between the Cs until your arm becomes used to the distance between these notes. Lead with your fingers, and let the hand and forearm follow.

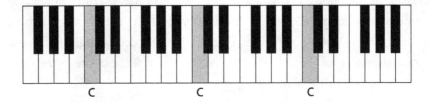

Once you feel comfortable with the distance between the Cs, start again at middle C and then play the G below middle C, return to middle C, and then play the G above. Alternate C, G, C, G until you master this shorter distance. This motion trains your forearm for a smaller beat pattern. Try using more force or energy for a louder sound and less energy for a softer sound, all the while keeping the size of the overall pattern the same.

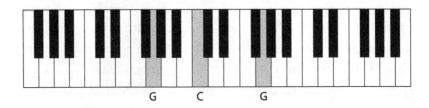

Bouncing Ball

To understand the feeling of impact and rebound that your hand and arm must show, instead of striking Cs on the piano, imagine that you are bouncing a basketball. Bounce the ball in front of your body, slightly to your right. This places the beat in a very natural position. The beat created by the bouncing basketball should be in line with your right leg and within the conducting strike zone area. The motion should not be located directly in the middle of your body because this position creates extra stress on the shoulder and arm.

CONDUCTING WITH THE HAND

Rounded Hand

When conducting with just your hand, make sure that your thumb is relaxed. Keep the palm of your hand downward and rounded, as if you were resting it lightly around a large grapefruit. Your fingers should be relaxed and slightly curved, not spread out or straight with tension. The quality of the sound when you conduct with your hand is influenced by the empty space in the hollow of your palm. To add buoyancy to the sound, imagine that

> **Conducting With The Hand**
>
> - Rounded Hand
> - Flat Hand
> - Thumb and Forefinger Touching
>
> **Video 3.5**

a stream of energy continually lifts the palm of your hand lightly from underneath, similar to air blowing up from a heater vent on the floor.

Flat Hand

Occasionally, you might want to use a flatter position of your hand to create more contact with the sound. Practice the motion of wiping off the table in front of you, perhaps with a polishing rag or pad. As you do this, your hand becomes flatter and the fingers straighten out creating more contact with the surface of the table. Instead of just the tip of the fingers being in contact with the sound, all the fingers are touching the table. This gesture creates a connected, sustained sound and you can vary the weight and resistance of this motion. As you increase the pressure of your fingers on the imaginary table, you will achieve an even deeper quality of sound. This flatter hand position is good for smooth legato passages involving louder dynamic levels.

Thumb and Forefinger Touching

When conducting with just the hand, some people like to utilize a position where the thumb and forefinger are touching. This hand position is effective for articulated passages, or cues. Holding the hand in this manner gives a clearer point of attack or entrance to the ensemble. When you conduct with this hand position, you will utilize mainly hand/wrist motion, while holding your forearm and arm still.

With this hand technique, make sure that the little finger is tucked in and not sticking straight up. When it is straight up, it can create a secondary impact point, and subconsciously send signals that may confuse the members of the ensemble.

As you can see, there is not a singular position for your hand while you are conducting. You must master a variety of hand positions and learn which ones are the most effective for each type of musical sound. With practice, you will be able to move easily from each of these hand positions to communicate the desired musical textures.

CONVEYING PULSE

One of the most important skills of being a good conductor is developing a strong inner sense of rhythm. This requires not just understanding the basic meters of the piece you are conducting, but also tuning in to the inner subdivisions of the pulse. When you conduct, you must constantly be mentally subdividing into 8th-notes, 16th-notes, and more. It is during this time between the major beats that the connection to the musical sound happens.

Practice subdividing inner beats in your mind as you train your muscles to maintain an established pulse. You must be able to isolate the movement of the fingers, the hand/wrist, the forearm, and the whole arm as you practice beating time.

Walking the Pulse

Because rhythm must be internalized, it is good to practice developing rhythmic precision while moving your body. Walk around the room with your feet stepping to the pulse of steady quarter notes. Keep the pulse slow to begin with. A pulse of quarter note = 60 works well. Gradually try walking faster while counting out a variety of meters. Do not just focus on the duple meter combinations; try also experimenting with meters of three, five, seven, and nine. Combine even meter groupings with odd meters as you walk. For this exercise, focus on stepping to the strong beats of each meter grouping.

INNER PULSE SUBDIVISIONS

Once you are comfortable with walking to the strong pulses, mentally start to add in the subdivisions of the pulse. As you continue to walk around the room to the strong beats, count internally: 1 *and* 2 *and* 1 *and* 2 *and*. Put the emphasis on the *and* of each beat. Strive to feel the inner rhythms more strongly than the main beats that you are pacing out.

After you acquire a good sense of the duple subdivision of each beat, try subdividing with a triple count for each main pulse. Count "*tri-pl-et, tri-pl-et*" silently as you walk. Then practice four subdivisions within each beat "*one-e and a two-e and a.*" Remember to keep your mental focus on the inner beats, not the main pulses. Now, count five subdivisions for each main pulse, or steps, with your feet "1*2345–*2*2345–*3*2345–*4*2345. Make sure that you keep your counting steady. Dividing one beat into five even subdivisions is particularly difficult.

When you are comfortable with subdivisions of five, advance to counting six subdivisions within each pulse. Try subdividing the beat three different ways: straight six by itself; then with a triple subdivision 1 2–3 4–5 6 or 1 *and*, 2 *and*, 3 *and*; then experiment with an inner duple subdivision 1 2 3–4 5 6. Try alternating between these three ways of breaking down meters of six pulses. You are essentially creating a larger beat pattern of one, two, or three.

Whole Measure Subdivisions

It is possible to divide groupings of 7, 8, and 12 into combinations of subdivisions that create different larger beat structures. A bar with eight sub-pulses can be organized into the standard four beat groupings of 2+2+2+2, or within a three-beat pattern such as 3+3+2, 2+3+3, 3+2+3. These alternate groupings will create an uneven step as you are walking these rhythms.

You can group seven-beat measures in a variety of combinations within a basic three pattern 3+2+2, 2+3+2, 2+2+3, and measures of 12 beats can be divided into either 3+3+3+3 creating four strong beats, or 4+4+4 for three main beats. Internalize the micro and the macro of each of these rhythmic pulses while you are marching to the strong beats.

Table Taps

To further internalize a sense of inner pulse, try tapping a consistent pulse to the beat of a metronome on a table with your fingers. Rest the forearm on the table and just lift up the fingers. Practice tapping with each finger, lifting each one up about one inch off the table each time. Feel the muscles of your forearm move and flex as you tap. Do not move the arm itself, just the fingers. Reset the metronome and practice tapping at different speeds. First practice tapping slowly and evenly to build control, then set the metronome on a faster tempo to develop more muscle strength and flexibility. Once you feel you have mastered this with the right hand, do the same motions with your left hand. (See Video 3.6. ▶)

WRIST MOTION

Now perform the same exercise with the hand/wrist action. Notice that the wrist itself does not move down or up. Instead, the flat part of your hand lifts upward. The motion stems from where the hand attaches to the wrist and the hand bends up. In this manner, the palm of the hand and the fingers are lifted slightly off the table and then put back down. The movement of this lift upward can be anywhere from one to about three inches. While you are performing this motion, your arm should remain still and relaxed, although some of your muscles will flex each time you lift your hand.

When you conduct using wrist motion, you want to experience this same feeling as if your hand and arm were resting on a table. Your wrist should stay even with the forearm and the hand must lift up from that joint, and then return to a level position. You should never conduct with the wrist bent upward and the hand dropping downward.

FOREARM MOTION

To focus on the motion of your forearm, tap steadily on the table by lifting your forearm off the table in one gesture, bending at the elbow, and then moving your forearm downward to tap with your fingertips on the table. The wrist and hand should stay in a straight line, even with the forearm and moving as one unit. Your metronome tempo will need to be slower for practicing this gesture because of the extended time it takes to lift your forearm off the table.

WHOLE ARM MOTION

Last, you will want to practice tapping on the table by using your whole arm, rotating from your shoulder. Your arm should be slightly bent at the elbow, and you can lift it in one continuous motion from the shoulder. With this gesture, you will be able to lift your hand much higher off the table and the beats you tap will be large and powerful. By practicing this motion, you will be able to develop the muscles in your shoulder and back, training them for occasions when you want to evoke a loud, forceful sound from your ensemble.

THE BATON

For beginning conductors, the use of the baton may feel awkward and disconnected. This is especially true for those who first learned to conduct using just the hand. Many conductors who believe that they are using the baton properly are actually still communicating to their ensemble through the *hand,* using the fingers or palm as the main focal point for conveying rhythm and pulse. When this happens, the tip of the baton is merely reacting and following the hand's impact. Unfortunately, this creates a double beat pattern, making it very difficult for the musicians to play accurately together. Showing pulse with your hand while also holding a baton is to be avoided, so it is important to learn and master proper baton technique.

Pencil Baton

To shift the energy from your hand to the tip of the baton, it is useful to start with something that is shorter, such as a pencil. Experiment with conducting with a very short pencil, just slightly longer than the length of your fingers. As you become used to the tip of your pencil being the focal point, not your fingers, you can gradually begin to use a longer pencil. When you feel completely confident that you are communicating energy through the tip of a full-length pencil, you can then switch to a real baton. (See Video 3.7. ▶)

You might find it much harder to convey weight and resistance with the slim stick of the baton than with your hand or with the pencil. Practice alternating between conducting with your right hand, your pencil, and then the baton until you are able to shift the focus consistently to the tip of the baton. This will enable you to communicate weight and resistance clearly.

Selecting a Baton

Over the years, the standardized lengths of conducting batons have changed dramatically. In photos of conductors from several decades ago, you will notice that their batons were quite long and the sticks thick and durable. Sometimes the length of a baton was up to 20 inches or more.

Now, conductors tend to gravitate toward batons that are between 12 and 15 inches long. Most are light and carefully balanced. Choose a length and balance that allows you to comfortably connect with the tip of the baton at all times. The length that feels right to you will be influenced by the length of your arms and the general size of your gestures.

Baton sticks can be made out of wood, fiberglass, graphite, carbon fiber, or titanium. Even though batons with a natural, unstained, wood stick are available, it is much easier for the players to see a baton that is white. With that in mind, you should also avoid wearing a solid white shirt while conducting because the musicians will not be able to see the baton against your clothing.

Baton Handles

The handles for conducting batons are usually made of wood, but they can also be made of cork, metal, rubber, or plastic. You should use whatever feels most comfortable in your hand. The baton handle should be smooth, but you also must be able to retain a good grip so it will not fly out of your hand while you are conducting.

Here are some of the better-known baton makers:

> Mollard (www.Mollard.com)
> Newland (www.Newlandbatons.com)
> Guy Lake (www. GLCustombatons.com)
> Conrad (www.Conradbatons)
> Old World (www.Oldworldbaton.com)

Many of these baton makers offer handles made out of a variety of beautiful and exotic woods. They give you choices of the shape of the handle, the weight and balance, and the length of the stick. Experiment to see what shape of handle feels good in your hand. If your hand is small, you should probably avoid the larger handles, while a person with a larger hand might need a bigger surface in their palm so that the baton does not wobble. Luckily, conducting batons are not as expensive as violins, so you can purchase and experiment with quite a few without great financial hardship.

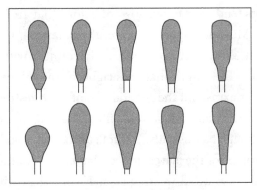

Baton Handles

Holding the Baton

Even if you are left-handed, it is important that you hold your conducting baton in your right hand. Violinists and cellists do not play their instruments backward just because one of their hands is more dominant than the other. As a conductor, you will utilize each of your hands differently and each hand will be trained specifically for its role. It does not matter that one hand might at first feel a little more natural with certain motions. With practice, either

> **Holding the Baton**
>
> • Standard Position
> • Cuing Position
> • Light Position
> • Underhand Position
> • Heavy Position
>
> **Video 3.8**

hand should feel equally at ease with all of the conducting gestures that you utilize.

There are several ways to hold the baton, and you must be able to switch between them. A relaxed and comfortable grip on your baton is necessary for communicating the essence of the music, but your basic hand positions will need to be adapted as you navigate different beat patterns and styles of music. Do not become trapped into thinking there is just one way to hold a baton. That would be similar to believing there is only one violin bow hold and technique. Yes, there are basic concepts and finger placement that should be followed, but flexibility of the fingers and a slight variety to the basic grip are necessary to communicate specific accents and articulations within each musical phrase.

STANDARD POSITION

There is, however, a standard baton grip that seems to be the most popular way to hold a conducting baton. The handle of the baton is held loosely in the palm of your hand, with your third finger (ring finger) anchoring the handle against the base of your thumb. The stick of the baton is held loosely between thumb and first finger. The thumb should be relaxed, but slightly bent. There will be a small, open circular space between the thumb and the first finger. The middle joint of your middle finger will also rest against the edge of the baton. The little finger should gently curl in next to the third finger. The handle of the baton will be near the base of the thumb, not over next to the little finger.

As you conduct with the baton, your hand will be in approximately the same position in front of your body as it was when you conducted without the baton, slightly to your right over your right foot. Your palm will be facing the floor with the top of your hand being flat. The tip of the baton will point forward, but slightly toward the center of your body, in an extended line following the natural position of your forearm.

As you work with your baton, do not let its handle slide to a position under the little finger. This type of position moves the baton in a sideways fashion and makes it difficult for the tip to point forward. The tip should always be in line with your forearm. This way, the baton can become an extension of your body.

CUING POSITION

Some conductors like to hold the baton so that their first finger is extended and resting on top of the stick. This type of position can reduce some of the normal mobility of the hand and fingers, but it can be effective for specific cuing when a very strong precise motion of the baton is desired. The motion tends to come from the wrist, and the baton functions as a pointer. With the finger on top of the baton, you are able to directly control the tip with very little bounce or rebound.

LIGHT POSITION

When you are conducting soft, light passages, try altering the way you hold your baton to allow for more flexibility of your fingers. This involves holding the baton just above the handle, forward in your palm, so that the stick is held loosely between the thumb and the first two fingers.

An open circle will be created between the handle and the palm of your hand. The handle of the baton will either float in this space or rest gently against your palm at the point where the first and second fingers connect to your hand. The fingers in this type of conducting position are much more active and flexible, which allows you to perform very small gestures with the baton tip.

UNDERHAND POSITION

There are also times when an underhand baton grip is appropriate. This is most effective for passages of music that are legato and flowing. The fingers will loosely hold the baton in the same manner as the light position;

however, the hand will be turned at the wrist and forearm so that the palm is now facing upward. This type of baton grip is performed close to the body and requires rounding and lowering your arms slightly. The conducting gesture utilizes movement from the wrist and forearm. It is a baton grip that is comfortable, flowing, and easy to execute.

HEAVY POSITION

For heavy, loud sections of music, experiment with holding the baton in a way that is similar to a handshake. The fingers are curled around the handle as before, but the hand is turned slightly to the side with the thumb on top. With this type of position, you can utilize the whole arm in a powerful downward stroke. This is excellent for single loud chords. This gesture is similar to the manner in which a fortissimo stroke is played on the timpani.

Developing Your Muscles

Holding a baton in your hand might at first feel awkward. It may take a while for your hand to adjust and for your muscles to develop so that you have a greater flexibility of motion. In the beginning you should carry a baton with you wherever you go. You can hold it while you are watching television, or while you are walking around your home. The baton needs to become a part of you.

As you hold your baton, make sure that you are able to connect to its point at all times. Tap it on objects and practice separating the movement of the fingers, hand/wrist, forearm, and full arm. While you are practicing, you can alternate between the different types of grips, but spend the most time on becoming comfortable with the standard grip.

Here are some other exercises to help strengthen your muscles. (See Video 3.9. ▶))

FINGER CRUNCHES

To strengthen the flexibility of your fingers, try practicing *finger crunches*. Without the baton, extend your thumb and your fingers out and together, then bend them and pull them toward your palm. Do this over and over until the motion of your fingers becomes fluid. Keep the thumb and the forefinger touching lightly as you do this exercise. Feel how the muscles in your forearm must work to perform this exercise. Your goal is to strengthen those muscles.

WRIST CIRCLES

It is also good to practice performing small circles with your wrist. Remember, your hand must never drop lower than your forearm, so the motion is always upward and around. Wrist circles involve holding your baton in the standard grip and then rolling your hand upward from the wrist in small clockwise circles. As you do this, you will actually feel the muscle in your forearm near the elbow joint contract and release. Practicing these circles will help you to develop the strength of this specific muscle, which is needed for a variety of conducting techniques.

Focus on the Tip

When you are conducting with a baton, all energy connects to the music at the tip of the baton. This is a very important concept, and it is often misunderstood. You never want the tip of your baton to flap wildly. To keep the focus on the tip, remember our table of sound and our imaginary keyboard. Just as you should never lift your shoulders to strike a single key on the piano, you would not start a conducting gesture from the shoulder or the arms. The arms and shoulders help provide the weight and flow of the gesture, but the connection and action always come from the very tip of the baton.

Many conductors think they are conducting clearly simply because they are holding the baton correctly. Holding it correctly has nothing to do with the manner in which energy and pulse are being communicated to your ensemble. All too often, conductors are actually still conducting the pulse with their hand, not with the tip of the baton, creating a wavy beat that is unclear and frustrating to follow. It is difficult to change the focus of the energy to a point that is farther out from your body.

Think again of our table of sound. As you hold your baton and tap on your imaginary table of sound in front of you, sense the contact point as the baton touches the table. If you are still having trouble with this concept, sit in front of an actual table and tap it lightly with your baton. Feel the contact with the table. Focus on the relationship of the finger, hand, wrist, arm, and shoulders as they coordinate the motion of the baton tip.

If you are still having difficulty with connecting to the tip, experiment with holding your baton backward, with the end of the stick in your hand and the handle out toward your ensemble. You will immediately realize that the handle is much heavier than the stick. In this position, you are forced to focus on the tip area (now the handle) because the weight of the handle will be pulling downward continually. Beat a few patterns in this manner, then turn the baton around and conduct with it in the normal position. It should now be easier to connect to the tip of your baton.

Baton Taps

Baton taps are similar to table taps, but they are done in the air. Instead of starting with your hand resting on the table, the tip of the baton can tap on your imaginary table. In this case, the tip of the baton should tap at a point that is even with your hand and forearm. (See Video 3.10. ▶))

Finger Taps

You will want to isolate your muscle movements as you practice tapping with your baton. Start first with baton taps that are controlled solely by the fingers. For this you need to hold the baton with the "light grip" and your fingers and thumb will bend and flex as you move the baton through the air.

Hand/Wrist Taps

Once you are comfortable with moving your fingers freely, you can move on to baton taps controlled by the hand and wrist. The hand should always move upward from the wrist joint and then back down to be even with the wrist and arm as you practice these baton taps. Remember that the point of conveying pulse is still at the end of the baton, not at your wrist. As you do this, imagine that you are tapping on something sticky. Feel the contact point and the slight resistance at the tip of the baton.

Forearm Taps

Baton taps that use the forearm are a little harder to control. The contact point must still be at the tip of the baton, but the arm should bend at the elbow while the hand and wrist stay basically straight. There should be one line of communication from your elbow to the tip of the baton. As you tap a steady pulse while bending from the elbow, your wrist and fingers should remain relaxed and not locked.

BASIC CONDUCTING PATTERNS

Almost every conducting book contains diagrams showing the basic conducting patterns. The most famous book of conducting diagrams is by the legendary conductor Max Rudolph. With his diagrams, there are examples for each meter utilizing straight lines with an ictus to produce a more staccato, or marcato, sound, and curved lines to produce a legato, connected sound. Here are some examples of standard conducting patterns moving from staccato to legato. (See Video 3.11. ▶)

Standard Beat Pattern Diagrams

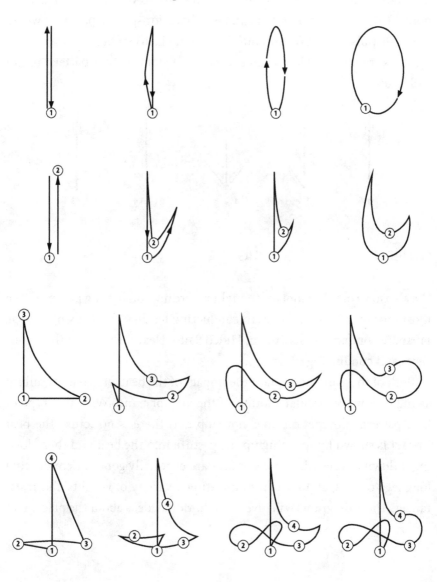

Patterns with All the Beats in the Center

The majority of conducting diagrams place the core beats of the measure separately, as displayed in the diagrams just shown. Beat one is in the middle, beats two and three are to each side, and beat four is in toward the center and upward from beat three. There are a few conducting methods, however, that advocate that all beats go through a center focal point. This is a technique that can be utilized for specific passages where the basic pulse is important, but the actual clarity of beats two or three is not as important. Here is an example of what this beat pattern might look like.

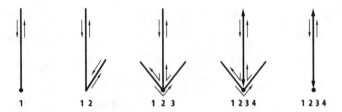

OTHER CONDUCTING SCHOOLS

We also have other schools of thought regarding conducting patterns. The most prominent are the Russian conducting teacher, Ilya Musin, and the Japanese conducting instructor, Hideo Saito. Next are some of their concepts and conducting diagrams.

Both of these methods place the impact of the beat within a pendulum swing or a more circular motion of the arm or hand. With this type of beat pattern, the motion does not stop and there is no ictus. The beat impact is shown by speeding up the gesture into the beat and then slowing it down afterward. These gestures are especially good for conducting long legato lines, and for communicating a variety of weights and resistances. These diagrams will give you additional ideas about the placement of conducting beat patterns and the diverse types of gestures that can be used to communicate music.

Circular Beat Patterns Based on "Picking Up the Sound" (Russian—Musin)

The Russian system of conducting developed by Ilya Musin is based upon circular motions in which you pull energy from one beat to the next. They refer to this as *picking up the sound*. The impact with the beat is always slightly delayed and with this method, you will feel like you are conducting slightly ahead of the ensemble. (See Video 3.12. ▶)

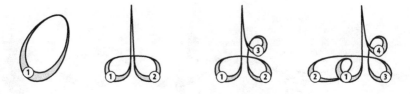

Arc and Pendulum Beat Patterns (Japanese—Saito)

The conducting method developed by Hideo Saito uses a pendulum swing or arc for legato gestures; straight strokes for staccato gestures; and motions that focus energy toward each beat, where you speed up as you move to the beat, and slow down during the rebound after the beat. With this method, you will notice that the placement of the main beats are very different from that of the standard beat patterns introduced earlier and that the diagrams are also quite different in their shape. Having knowledge of these diverse patterns will enhance your ability to communicate musical concepts to the musicians. (See Video 3.13. ▶)

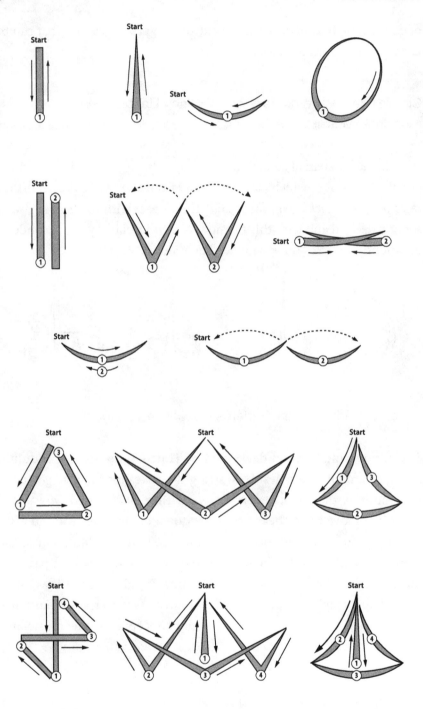

All in One Place (Japanese—Saito)

When using gestures from the Saito conducting method, it is also possible to show a pattern where all of the beats go through the center. This would be utilized for music that has a strong rhythmic feel, but does not require the players to distinguish the individual beats within the phrase.

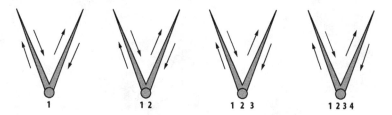

Subdivided Beat Patterns

Conducting with a subdivided beat pattern involves showing clearly the inner parts of the beats. It is important that the "sub" beats are smaller and have less energy than the strong beats so that your performers do not become confused. Sub-beats should not utilize an ictus. They are often used in a slower tempo to mark the inner pulse, or in a faster tempo to give more rhythmic clarity. (See Video 3.14. ▶)

2 Pattern – Subdivided

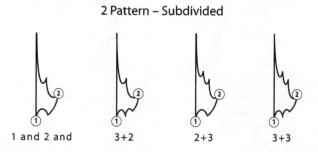

3 Pattern – Subdivided

5

2+2+1   1+2+2
2+1+2

6

2+2+2

7

   2+3+2
3+2+2   2+2+3

8

   2+3+3
3+3+2   3+2+3

9

3+3+3

4 Pattern – Subdivided

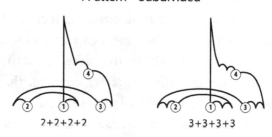

2+2+2+2   3+3+3+3

Mixed-Meter Patterns

Much of the music written before 1900 is in standard meter divisions that stay consistent throughout each piece. As composers started to write more complex rhythms that required different meter markings, the conductor's job became more difficult. Now we must be able to navigate easily between different meter patterns with a clarity that can be seen and properly interpreted by all of the ensemble members.

Conducting mixed-meter patterns requires the ability to vary the height and speed of the motions involved. If all of the gestures are the same height, the musicians cannot distinguish which beat is which. You must be sure that the first beat, the *one* beat, or downbeat, is always larger than the other beats so that musicians can look up at a glance and know where they are.

Practice conducting through the following example, making sure that the first beat of each bar is clearly delineated. Do this a few times utilizing different metronome markings, both slow and fast. Mixed-meter sections should never be conducted with all of the beats going through the center. It is important for you to exaggerate the placement of each of the beats in a mixed-meter pattern so that the ensemble will always know where you are in the measure.

Compound Meters

The difficulty of conducting mixed meters is increased when some beats have inner divisions of two sub-beats and others have inner divisions of three sub-beats within the same bar. This means that some beat gestures are actually of greater duration than others. To make your gestures effective, you will have to conduct the longer beat slightly slower than the beat with fewer subdivisions. You must be able to adjust the speed of the beat in a manner that does not convey a change in tempo.

It is also important that you conduct mixed-meter passages with a dry and clear beat. Too much rebound or ictus can be confusing to the musicians when you are conducting difficult, rhythmic passages. Use more hand/wrist motion, and less arm motion. A gesture that is small and rhythmically accurate, and clearly indicates a stopping point with each motion, is the clearest way of conducting mixed meters.

Here are some examples to practice for conducting uneven, mixedmeter patterns. Choose how you are going to divide these groupings. A five-beat pattern can be conducted as 2+3 or 3+2. Usually, this is dictated by the way the notes are barred and connected in the music itself. Sometimes you will need to explain to your musicians how you are grouping your subdivisions. This might be necessary if you are conducting in a pattern that conflicts with the specific markings or note groupings in some of the parts.

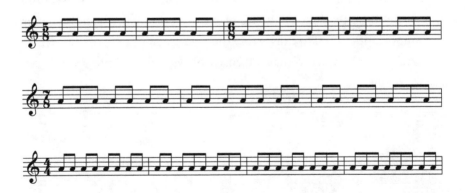

MARKING MIXED-METER PATTERNS

When you are conducting a score with numerous mixed-meter changes at a very fast tempo, it is important that you mark your score so that you can quickly remember how you are dividing these beat patterns. Most conductors use a system of small diagrams written above the staff. The following symbols can be used for these types of markings. It is important to develop a consistent system for marking your scores.

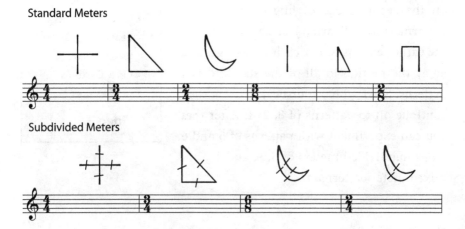

Standard Meters

Subdivided Meters

BEGINNING A MIXED-METER PASSAGE

When you are stopping and starting while rehearsing a section of music, you may find that you want to begin on a passage that is in a 5/8 meter, a 7/8 meter, or a beat pattern that is uneven. To give the proper preparation beat you will have to decide whether you give a pick-up beat with two subdivisions or three subdivisions. As a general rule, you should give a pick-up beat that is *equal to the largest grouping of subdivisions within the first measure.* For example, if you are showing the preparatory beat for a measure in 5/8 time, your pick-up beat would contain three inner beats, not two.

BATON EXERCISES

Merging Gestures into Patterns

We will now combine some of the gesture concepts introduced earlier in the book and apply them to basic conducting patterns. These will need to be practiced with a focus on the separate use of fingers, hand/wrist, forearm, and full arm, just as we did with the earlier exercises. For each type of gesture, apply the motion to all of the standard beat patterns. Start with a four-beat pattern, then, continue on to patterns of 3, 2, 1. After that, you can experiment with patterns of 5 and 6, larger subdivided meters of 8, 9, and 12, and mixed-meter patterns.

> **Merging Gestures into Patterns**
>
> • Ictus Gestures
> • Legato Gestures
> • Beats in the Center
> • Inactive Beats
> • Circle Gestures
> • Arc Gestures
>
> **Video 3.15** ▶

ICTUS GESTURES

	motion size	volume	mood/texture
Shaking drops of water off your baton	small	piano	light
Tapping a small nail with a hammer	medium	mezzo-forte	insistent
Hitting a larger nail with a hammer	large	forte	determined
Hitting a drum	very large	fortissimo	forceful

LEGATO GESTURES

Wiping away smudges with your baton	small	piano	touch
Spreading butter on bread	medium	mezzo-piano	contact
Ironing clothes	large	forte	resistance
Dragging a towel across a pool	very large	fortissimo	weight

Beats in the Center with Ictus

Tapping the table in the same place	small	piano	delicate
Playing with a paddle ball	medium	mezzo-piano	persistent
Bouncing a tennis ball	large	mezzo-forte	springy
Bouncing a basketball	very large	forte	bouncy

Inactive-Beat Gestures

Put your hand down on your imaginary table and simply move it to the left, then move it to the right, and then pick it up. The gesture must not have any energy attached to it. Practice this with both large and small movements, and adjust your motions to fit within different beat pattern. (See Video 3.16. ▶)

Circle Gestures

A circular gesture has a point of contact and release. There is also a feeling of increasing resistance as you move through to the impact or contact point, and a release of energy after this point. Practice these gestures utilizing standard conducting patterns. Experiment with placing the beats out to each side, and also with beats all going through the center.

Petting a bird	small	piano	gentle
Petting a cat	medium	mezzo-forte	comforting
Petting a large dog	large	forte	firm
Brushing a horse	very large	fortissimo	strong

Arc Gestures

Conducting arc patterns will require you to vary the speed of the gesture. You must show the acceleration toward the point of the beat or the bottom of the pendulum swing. This is then followed by a deceleration after that point to the end of the swinging motion.

To use this motion within a basic four-beat conducting pattern, you must communicate a sense of impact, yet never stop at the point where the beat occurs. Here are some examples to practice arc gestures.

Beat 1   Dipping your fingers in water and scooping some water out
Beat 2   Swinging your hand like a pendulum, to the left
Beat 3   Swinging your hand in a large arc, like a pendulum, to the right
Beat 4   Scooping and lifting some water

To show the inner pulse of subdivided beats, you can use smaller arc gestures like lightly following the rebounds of a small bouncing ball, or tracing the outline of a children's Christmas tree.

Other Beat Placement Concepts

There are a few other concepts that you will need to incorporate into your conducting technique that will influence how the musicians respond to your gestures. These are the *size* of the beat, the *height* of the beat, and the *placement* of the beats in relationship to your body.

SIZE OF THE BEAT
Usually a correlation exists between the size of the beat pattern and the volume that the ensemble will produce. The standard rule is that a large beat pattern will encourage the group to play loudly, while a small beat pattern will signal them to play softer.

The size of the beat, however, can also be related to the tempo. You will want to use a larger beat to show a slow tempo and a smaller beat to convey a fast tempo. The distance your hand must travel makes this necessary, since the speed your hand moves in a specific tempo should stay consistent within the beat pattern.

HEIGHT OF THE BEAT
The height placement of the conducting pattern can be used in a variety of ways to affect the sound. Some conductors will use a high placement of the beat pattern for a soft musical passage and a low beat pattern for a loud section. You can also use the height of the beat to affect the quality or fullness of the sound. For example, a higher beat can be used for light

passage work and a lower beat for thick, sustained passages. Some conductors use the height of the beat pattern to reflect the contour, or pitch level, of a specific passage, conducting "higher" when the notes on the page are written higher, and much lower for a passage with a low tessitura.

DISTANCE FROM THE BODY

The distance of the beat from your body should also be taken into consideration as you are conducting. If you conduct very closely to your body, you may be sending subconscious signals of wanting the music to be softer or more intimate. Sometimes this position may also encourage musicians to play a passage more lightly, or with more transparency. In comparison, when you conduct with your hands and arms extended farther than usual from your body, the resulting sound may be heavier. When it is combined with a larger beat pattern, this gesture is used to illicit more volume, or to inspire louder playing.

RIGHT- AND LEFT-HAND INDEPENDENCE

Throughout this section of the book, we have basically been focusing on the motions of the right hand. It is now time to bring the left hand into the equation so that both hands can learn to work together. It is often said that the right hand communicates the tempo, the pulse, and the basic beat structure, and that the job of the left hand is to convey character, emotions, and cues to the performers.

The Left Hand

When a right-handed person begins to study conducting, the left hand will often feel awkward and stiff. Extra time should be spent developing the muscles of the left hand so that it will move with the same smoothness and fluidity of the right hand. If your dominant hand is your left hand, you might experience the same issues with the training of your right hand.

> **The Left Hand**
>
> • Downward
> • Upward
> • Side to Side
>
> **Video 3.17** ▶

Once fluidity is achieved in both hands, it is important that the hands are able to move completely independently of each other, and that the left hand does not simply mirror the right. This separation of motion does not happen by accident. At first, you will find it difficult to direct one hand to perform one gesture while the other is doing something completely different. Often, conductors stop too early in their practical training and never fully develop the independence of the hands that is necessary for successful conducting. Instead, their left hand tends to just follow along with the motions of their right hand. It is important to practice using your hands separately, and together, until you have mastered the physical gestures and muscle memory that allow them each to do their specific jobs.

Downward and Upward

The first step with the left hand is to master downward and upward gestures. These are especially important motions because you will use them to communicate a variety of dynamic levels and intensity.

To train your left hand, stretch it out in front of your body as if you were going to shake hands with someone, then gradually move your hand slowly and evenly up and down in front of your body, slight to the left side. Practice this exercise first with your palm down, and then do the same motions with the palm facing upward. Try to avoid bumps or stops within the gesture.

While you are practicing this up-and-down motion with your left hand, conduct a basic "four" pattern with your right hand. Make sure that your hands do not run into each other. Your hands should never cross in front of your body. Be careful not to stop the constant motion of the left hand whenever the right hand marks a beat. The motion of the left hand should always be fluid and smooth.

As you strengthen the independence of your left hand, be sure to practice the following gestures. These are motions that will often be used when conducting with the left hand.

MOTION DOWNWARD—WITH A STOP
To show a long smooth diminuendo

Sliding a dimmer switch down	short
Closing a Jack-in-the-Box toy	medium
Pulling down a window shade	long
Running your fingers down a fence	longer

MOTION UPWARD—WITH A STOP
To show a long smooth crescendo

Sliding a dimmer switch up	short
Lifting the foam off a bubble bath	medium
Lifting up a window from underneath	long
Running your fingers upward against a fence	longer

While utilizing both downward and upward motions with your left hand, experiment with showing different amounts of weight, going from a perception of no weight to a very heavy weight. These types of gestures can be used to communicate or affirm changes in dynamics, or to show musical tension and release.

Side to Side

Once you are comfortable with vertical gestures, experiment with moving your left hand horizontally from side to side. Once again, you can do this gesture with your palm either up or down. The important aspect is to keep your hand constantly moving. The turn-around motion at the end of each gesture should be smooth and fluid. Once you become more comfortable with these side-to-side motions, add the right hand conducting a variety of meter patterns at the same time. As you are practicing, keep your left-hand gesture slightly to the left side of your body so your hands will not cross.

Motion sideways, flat plane
To show a long melodic phrase (both directions—palm down)

Running your fingers lightly across a table   light
Tracing a dome arc slowly in the air   light

Motion sideways, with weight, flat plane
To show a long phrase with a crescendo (hand turned sideways)

Pushing something away with the back of your hand   medium
Dragging a wet towel across a pool   heavy

Motion sideways, with resistance, flat plane
To show a long phrase with a diminuendo

Drawing your hand across the top of water   medium
Pulling a pile of coins toward you   medium

Earlier in the book, we talked about the horizontal wall plane directly in front of you. Conducting on this plane with an open palm directly out facing the musicians tends to convey a negative, almost policeman-like stance. It does not encourage the players to play and should be avoided.

Combining Directions and Patterns

As you work to develop the independence of your hands, explore conducting a variety of side-to-side and up-and-down gestures with your left hand, while your right hand conducts a series of beat patterns. Write out a list of mixed-meter measures on a piece of paper that you can follow, or practice the following example. This can help you develop the visual tracking skills that are required for conducting, while also greatly improving your ability to separate the actions of the right and left hands.

POSTER DRAWING

Another way to increase the independence of your left hand is to take a large piece of paper (17" × 11" or larger) and draw a squiggly pattern on it that connects to itself. The lines can overlap and move all over the page. In the end, your drawing might look something like this:

When you have finished your drawing, tape it to a wall in front of you at about chest level. Center your drawing in front of your left arm. Make sure that as you stand in front of this picture, you can easily touch the drawing with your fingers. Now, carefully trace this pattern with the fingers of your left hand, moving your hand slowly and continuously as you trace the lines. Once your left hand feels in control of the pattern, add the right hand conducting a variety of meters while you continue to trace the picture with your left hand. Start with simple meter patterns of two, three, and four, and then try more complex meter combinations. You can use a metronome to help establish a steady pulse.

To make things more challenging, experiment with conducting larger and smaller beat patterns with your right hand while keeping the left hand slowly and continuously following your "squiggle" diagram. You can even try some mixed-meter patterns with the right hand. This exercise will help you establish more control over the independent movements of both your hands.

Once you are comfortable with basic beat patterns, mixed-meter gestures, and the independence of your right and left hands, you are ready to move on to the more complex concepts of communicating specific musical ideas through the application of gestures to which you have already been introduced.

Applying and Combining Gestures

STARTING THE ENSEMBLE

Directing a group of musicians to begin playing together is like landing an airplane. If you do not execute it just right, it can be very bumpy and uncomfortable. Sometimes it can even crash. To ensure a safe, clean musical beginning, you must first make sure that you have the ensemble's full attention.

The Pause

Before you begin conducting, pay careful attention to the level of sound in the room. If it is not yet silent, do not start. Wait for complete quiet. This moment, that I call *the pause*, is very important for focusing the attention and energy of the group so that they will perform well together.

During this pause, observe the members of the ensemble and strive to tune in to the energy and mood in the room. What are they thinking? What are they feeling? This silence before you start the music is important for establishing the essence of the sound. It is the starting point for everything that happens in a rehearsal or a concert. Sometimes, the musicians will need more time to get ready. As you allow them this time, stand on the podium and quietly wait. Do not fidget, turn pages, or bury your head in the score. Help to center their attention by your calm demeanor. Allow everyone in the room the time they need to focus before the music making begins; this level of attention will carry over to the rest of the rehearsal.

The Prep Beat

Conductors sometimes find it difficult to give a steady preparatory beat to set the tempo and mood for the beginning of a piece. Remember that the *prep beat is always one full beat before the first note of the piece*. Therefore, if the piece starts on beat one, then your hand should start at the impact point for beat four. If the piece starts on beat two, your hand would start at beat one. It is essential that you show at least one full beat before the music begins.

The prep beat must indicate the exact tempo of the piece. To ensure this, it is helpful to count a full measure of beats silently in your head before showing your preparatory beat. To establish the tempo in your mind, focus on the melody of a more involved section of the piece to make sure you are not setting the opening tempo either too fast or too slow. During the motion of your actual prep beat, internalize the inner subdivisions of the pulse by counting a triplet subdivided beat. This will keep you from rushing your gesture before the first entrance. It is also important to im-agine the sound you want to hear and to make sure that your preparatory gesture sets up the attack and sound quality.

You must feel a connection to the sound you want to hear *before* your hand moves to give the preparatory beat. This is where the feeling of weight and resistance that we spoke about earlier must be practiced and clearly conveyed. The tip of the baton should feel as if it is lifting some-thing, or pulling away from something, during your preparatory beat gesture. This resistance will create a connection to the sound before you start. Your gesture will have substance, which will enable it to evoke a specific tone color and volume from the ensemble.

Always breathe in tempo as you conduct your preparatory beat. This will encourage your performers to breathe with you. Your timed breath allows the musicians to articulate the first note more clearly, so that they will be able to play or sing together with ease.

As you practice starting the ensemble, remember that the shorter the preparatory beat, the better the chance that the group will play together. By "shorter," I am referring to distance, not speed. When you are using a short stroke for a fast preparatory beat, you may actually have to wait a second before you give the actual entrance beat. When this happens, it is even more important for you to be subdividing and counting, so that you do not rush from the preparatory beat into the downbeat.

PRACTICING PREP BEATS

As you practice giving preparatory beats, understand that they will start from different positions, depending upon the beginning of the piece. This means that some preparatory beats will be within a vertical gesture, while others will be shown on the horizontal plane. Some will require you to combine a vertical gesture with a horizontal one. Horizontal and vertical motions require different muscles, and you must practice moving smoothly between these gestures. The following exercises will help you practice conducting different preparatory beats.

PREPARING FOR ONE—VERTICAL GESTURE

The preparatory beat for conducting an entrance on beat one must be connected to weight and energy. Experiment with showing different types of weight as you practice this preparatory gesture to beat one. (See Video 4.1. ▶))

Wet Rag

Rest the tip of your baton on your table of sound in front of you, then lift your baton tip as if you were raising a wet rag, a distance of about eight inches, then put it down again. Feel the imaginary weight at the tip of your baton. This is how you must connect to the sound as you prepare to give the downbeat. Practice this gesture again, breathing in as you lift, and breathing out as your hand comes back down. The ensemble will play when your hand comes down. Now, imagine that the wet rag is smaller and lighter. How will this affect the quality or fullness of the entrance?

Button

Perform the same gesture again, but this time, pretend that you are lifting a coat button with the tip of your baton. As you lift, count to three using the triplet subdivision then place the button back on your table of sound. What type of sound and musical attack would this gesture produce? Can you hear it in your head?

Ball of Cotton

For an even lighter preparatory beat, imagine that there is a ball of cotton on your table of sound. Pick it up with the tip of your baton. Connect to it and feel its lightness. Try experimenting with prep beats of different tempos while picking up this ball of cotton and placing it down again on your table of sound. Focusing on a physical object can give more substance to each of your gestures and enables you to connect to the musicians and the music.

PREPARING FOR TWO—VERTICAL THEN HORIZONTAL GESTURE

When you have an entrance that begins on beat two, the preparatory beat takes place on beat one. Here are some gestures to train your hand to show this type of preparatory beat. (See Video 4.2. ▶)

Window Shade—Wiping Dust

When the preparatory beat is given on beat one to prepare for an entrance on beat two, you must start with your hand held very high. To connect to the sound, imagine that you are pulling down on the tab of a window shade. Once the window shade is pulled down to your table of sound, let it go and let your hand bounce up slightly with the rebound while you breathe in for the prep; then wipe the dust off the table with a motion of your hand to either the left or the right, depending upon whether you are in a four-beat pattern or a three-beat pattern.

Closing the Trunk—Sliding Rocks

For a heavier sound or entrance, hold your hand up high, as if it is on the lifted hood or trunk of a car. Now press down, feeling the resistance as you close this hood. Feel your hand bounce back up slightly as the hood closes and you release your pressure. Make sure that you breathe in with the release of your hand. Follow this with a gesture to either side, imagining that you are pushing a heavy pile of rocks off your table of sound with the tip of your baton. Feel the resistance as you make this motion.

PREPARING FOR THREE—HORIZONTAL GESTURE

Pieces or phrases that begin on beat three will require a preparatory beat on beat two. The following gestures can be used to show this preparatory beat. (See Video 4.3. ▶)

Rubber Band—Painting a Line

To show the preparatory beat for an entrance on beat three within a standard four-beat pattern, you must start with your hand in the middle. Grab the end of an imaginary rubber band and breathe in as you stretch it to your left. Feel the tension and resistance. Once the rubber band is stretched, release it, and then draw a painting stroke across your body, level with your table of sound, as if you are painting a line on a wall or chalkboard, or brushing your hand across the top of a table. Feel the differences in the two gestures. One has resistance, the other a feeling of release.

Back-Handed Tennis Stroke

For a louder entrance, you need to show a stronger motion utilizing more speed and resistance. Start again with your hand in the middle, but now imagine that you are pulling your hand to your left side and your baton is like a tennis racket. Breathe in as you pull your hand and arm across your body. Notice the slight pause before the hand swings back across your body to the right. As you swing, focus on the impact point with "the ball." This is the entrance point for the musicians, followed by a continuation of the motion in the same direction. The gesture energy moves toward this contact point and then releases.

PREPARING FOR FOUR—HORIZONTAL THEN VERTICAL GESTURE

When you want to show a preparatory beat before beat four, this motion is shown on beat three. Remember that you must always connect to the weight, energy, and resistance of the motion in order to convey the quality of sound desired. (See Video 4.4. ▶)

Rubber Band—Wine Glass Toast

To prepare for an entrance on beat four (or in a three pattern, on beat three), you can use the rubber band concept again, only this time, start in the middle and stretch the rubber band to the right side. Make sure you remember to breathe in and to count a triplet rhythm as you give this gesture. Once you have reached the outward point of your motion, imagine that you are holding a wine glass in your hand and lift it up toward the center of your body, as if you are proposing a toast. The sound will occur as you grasp and begin to lift the glass. Feel the weight of the glass in your hand as you lift it up. Experiment with a full glass, a glass that contains less liquid, and one that is empty. Imagine the variety of sound qualities that would be produced with each different weight.

Bag of Rocks—Ice Cube Scoop

To inspire an even louder sound, experiment with pulling a heavy bag of rocks to the right on top of your table of sound as you breathe in; then, with an imaginary large scoop in your right hand, lift up a pile of frozen ice cubes. Feel how this weight perception differs from that of a single wine glass.

Extra Prep Beat

It is sometimes necessary to give two preparatory beats before beginning a piece. This is done when a piece is in a fast tempo that might be hard to start with just one beat. This extra gesture helps communicate the tempo and allows the wind players and vocalists to breathe more effectively, so that the entrance is together. When giving two preparatory beats, the first must be without energy or ictus. To become comfortable with showing two prep beats, practice the following gestures. (See Video 4.5. ⏵)

Two Prep Beats

Entrances on One

Conduct an entrance on beat one, with two prep beats and a sharp accent:

| Prep | Wipe off the table to your right (without energy—passive) |
| Prep | Lift a salt shaker while breathing in (thinking a triplet subdivision of the beat) |

Entrance   Throw the salt shaker down on the table, releasing your hold and your breath

Conduct an entrance on beat one, with two prep beats and no accent:

Prep   Wipe off the table to your right (without energy—passive)
Prep   Lift the salt shaker while breathing in
Entrance   Gently put the salt shaker back down and breathe out

Entrances on Two
Conduct an entrance on beat two, with two prep beats:

Prep   From resting your hand on your imaginary table slightly to the right of your body, put your finger in the air near the center of your body, as if you are going to ask a question (passive)
Prep   Pull the window shade down; release it with a rebound and a breath
Entrance   Sweep your hand to the left or right to brush off the table, and release your breath

Entrances on Three
Conduct an entrance on beat three, with two prep beats:

Four-beat Pattern

Prep   Start with your hand elevated in the center, then place it down on the table (passive)
Prep   Pull a rubber band to the left while breathing in
Entrance   Wipe the table while moving your hand to the right, releasing your breath

Three-beat Pattern

Prep   From the elevated position of your hand, place it down on the table (passive)
Prep   Pull a rubber band to the right while breathing in
Entrance   Pick up a wine glass for a toast

Entrances on Four

Conduct an entrance on beat four, with two prep beats:

Prep	Start in the middle with your hand on the table of sound and wipe the table to the left (passive)
Prep	Pull rubber band all the way to the right while breathing in
Entrance	Lift the wine glass up

The Entrance

As you start your preparatory beat, you are communicating the attack and sound of the first note by the type of motion you are using. The size of your beat will influence both the volume and the character of the sound. The speed, placement, and impact of the beat will define the articulation. Do you want a soft, spongy sound where your hand simply sinks into your table of sound? Or do you want a sharp, precise entrance that requires a clear ictus utilizing a tap and a rebound motion? The articulation of the first note and the volume level you wish to achieve are all communicated through the preparatory gesture before the entrance.

ARTICULATED ENTRANCES

Short, accented entrances are created by utilizing motions with an ictus and a sharp rebound. These entrances can be performed in a variety of dynamic levels, going from *pp* to *ff*. Each motion listed below has its own naturally connected preparatory gesture. These gestures can be used for any of the beats within your conducting pattern. In general, they move downward in direction, or they can be performed with a forward motion. Practice giving articulated entrance gestures utilizing the following motions. (See Video 4.6. ▶)

Forte—Downward
- Bouncing a basketball
- Hammering a nail on a table

Piano—Downward

- Playing with a yo-yo
- Playing a piano

Forte—Forward

- Cracking a whip
- Hammering a nail into a wall

Piano—Forward

- Throwing a dart
- Tapping on a wall

Smooth Entrances

For legato passages, you must use a gesture that connects the motion between the beats. Instead of bouncing and rebounding, your gesture should communicate that you are picking up an item with a perceived weight and moving it to the next beat. This is shown by using a more circular motion around each beat point. Within this gesture, you must establish a connection to perceived weight and resistance, and maintain continuous contact with the sound. (See Video 4.7. ▶)

Forte—Side to Side

- Picking up a heavy rock and moving it to either side
- Pulling your hand downward through mud, scooping it up and moving it to either side

Mezzo-forte—Side to Side

- Picking up a handful of dirt and moving it to another pile
- Picking up a salt shaker and moving it to either side

Piano—Side to Side

- Picking up a marble and moving it to either side
- Picking up a pea and moving it to either side
- Picking up a piece of rice and moving it to either side

You can also use a pendulum-swinging motion to conduct legato entrances and legato passages of music. With this gesture, the impact of the beat occurs in the middle of the gesture, similar to hitting a tennis ball, not at the end of the stroke like an ictus entrance. Most of these gestures move sideways and horizontally. You will need to show a slight pressing motion as you pass through each beat point.

Forte—Pendulum Swing
- Swinging a tennis racket
- Swinging a sword

Mezzo-forte—Pendulum Swing
- Petting a dog
- Petting a rabbit

Piano—Pendulum Swing
- Petting a bird
- Petting a mouse

PRESSED ENTRANCES
Certain music requires that the sound be sunken into, or *pressed*. With this type of gesture, there is no sharp, clear attack, but rather the sound begins and then swells a little as the contact increases. Motions that elicit this type of pressed musical entrance include the following. (See Video 4.8. ▶)

- Touching a ball of cotton
- Pressing down on a wet sponge
- Pressing gently on a pillow
- Rolling a rolling pin (two hands)

The Delay

For a beginning conductor, one of the hardest things to become accustomed to is that the sound from your ensemble will always seem a fraction behind the actual impact of your gesture. This is a result of the response time necessary for a large group to react to your motion. In Europe, this delayed sound has even become a tradition. The larger the rebound motion in your gesture, the more the sound will be delayed.

It is important that you do not react to the delayed sound, or in any way slow down your gestures to "be with the ensemble." Instead, you must always conduct slightly ahead of the sound you are hearing, and continuously lead the group. During your first conducting experiences, you might find this difficult, but eventually you will master it. If you do not conduct slightly ahead, not only will the group begin to play slower and slower, but they will also stop watching you. Eventually, you will end up following *them*, and very little real music making will happen.

CONTROLLING THE SOUND

Conducting is all about shaping musical sounds, developing the technique to control the articulation of the sound, and understanding how sound is produced by the various instruments or voices. A strong foundation in instrumental and vocal characteristics and limitations will help you select the most appropriate gesture for your conducting, thus enabling the musicians to perform better.

Instrument Characteristics

Each family of instruments produces sound differently and therefore benefits from a unique type of gesture for cues and entrances.

WOODWIND INSTRUMENTS

Entrances
Double-reed instruments, such as oboes and bassoons, will always need a very strong ictus beat on their entrances, so that the sound of their instruments will speak. Their reeds require a forceful breath from the musician and a clear tonguing technique.

Flute players need a clear placement of the sound with a good breath, but not so much of a sharp ictus. A pressed type of beat gesture works well for their entrances, unless their parts indicate accented notes.

Single-reed instruments like clarinets and saxophones do not need an ictus at all, unless they are playing an entrance with an accent. They can sneak in, even when given a very smooth gesture.

Difficult Notes

Low notes in the flutes tend to have difficulty projecting through the ensemble. Be aware of this problem as you are rehearsing and balancing a section. Even if you ask them to play louder in their low register, it is just not possible on their instrument.

Low notes in the oboes are difficult to perform in tune and softly. Be understanding of your oboe players when they are in their lowest range. They might not be able to play as softly as you would like because of the limitations of the instrument.

Bassoons sometimes tend to play slightly sharp. When tuning chords, it is standard procedure to tune from the bottom or the lowest instrument, but if you hear that your bassoons are playing sharp, then tune from the top or the middle of the chord, and have the bassoons match that pitch first. Once you are sure the pitch is stable, you can add in the other instruments.

BRASS INSTRUMENTS

Breath

Brass players need a good breath and also a clear ictus for them to play together. The lower the instrument is, the larger the gesture and preparatory breath that is needed. It requires a lot of air to produce an accurate entrance with a good tone quality on the tuba. Help your brass players to breathe and play together.

When you are working with brass players, instruct them that their breath between notes or phrases should never be taken out of the note that follows; instead the current note should be shortened to allow time for a quick breath. Otherwise, entrances and note changes will continually sound late.

Register

Low, legato brass notes tend to sound behind the rest of the ensemble because it takes a moment longer for the sound to be produced on the instrument. When performing low passages of music on brass instruments, make sure that the players anticipate the entrances of these notes. It helps for you to show the breath clearly to the section, and for you to anticipate this possible delay.

Large interval leaps in the brass also tend to be difficult to produce. Help your musicians with these passages by continuing to move in time to the next beat and by not allowing the music to drag.

Seating

Because many of the brass performers sit at the back of the rehearsal room or stage, it may be difficult for them to see the beat clearly or to hear your instructions. Be aware of these issues as you conduct. Speak loudly, and make sure that your beat is large enough when the brass section is playing.

This extended distance from the podium and the audience will also affect the brass sound in the hall, sometimes causing it to be heard late. When this happens, use a smoother beat with less ictus to move the players faster to the next beat. Large rebound motions will always create a delay effect in the sound.

STRING INSTRUMENTS

When dealing with string instruments, you have two different types of sound production: bowed or plucked. Within the category of bowed attacks we have accented notes and entrances, legato notes and entrances, and a large variety of types of attacks and articulations that are between the two.

Legato Entrances and Attacks

String players can perform a legato entrance with very little motion from you as a conductor. The less clear you are, the softer and fuzzier the sound will be. This is especially useful if you want a very transparent sound. A pressed gesture is useful to show a legato string entrance; the more weight shown in the gesture, the louder the volume of the entrance.

Staccato Entrances and Attacks

When conducting staccato string entrances, you can use a strong ictus and rebound type of beat. Your gesture can actually imitate the way the string players place their bow on the string and the way they push, or press, to create an accented attack.

Other Bowed Entrances and Attacks

String players can perform heavy down-bow accents that are repeated, or up-bow staccato where all the notes are performed in one bow. They can also hook longer notes together in one bow but still have a slight separation of each note. When you conduct passages involving these types of articulations, your hand can show a motion similar to the way a string player pulls the bow. The more you work with string players, the more comfortable you will become in connecting to the variety of sounds that the bow produces.

Pizzicato Entrances

The motion for plucked sounds in the string section must be given very clearly. You will need to show a strong preparatory breath to ensure that all the players will pluck at the exact same time. The rebound motion of this gesture must also be clear to dictate the ring and release of the sound. You cannot be tentative when conducting pizzicato passages. Your musicians will need every pizzicato beat to be given clearly with an ictus and rebound, or they will not pluck together.

Tendency to Rush

Whenever string players have fast, difficult passages of 16th-notes, they will usually rush. To counter this, gradually use a larger, more legato beat, even if you are conducting an articulated passage. This type of gesture will prevent the string section from rushing because you will be more connected to the moving notes within the beats, and the distance that your hand travels will prohibit them from accelerating to the next beat too soon.

Vocal Characteristics

For singers, showing the breath is vitally important for starting the ensemble together and for creating a uniform sound. Strive to breathe with your group for all their entrances. As you rehearse your choir, you must be sure that you do not demonstrate any tension in your shoulder, face, hands, or body. Your choir members will subconsciously sense this tension and they will mirror your posture with their bodies. Body tension will create vocal problems and a forced sound quality.

Vocal Accents

The consonants in the words of a piece will usually create the effect of accented notes. You must be especially careful with the letters *s, sh, t,* and *z* because they tend to cut through the vocal texture if they are not produced absolutely together. These syllables must be conducted carefully with a clear ictus beat, followed by a precise release of the consonant sound.

Vocal Tone

A uniform vocal tone is achieved by making sure that the singers are vocalizing the exact same vowel sounds. Primary vowels such as *ay, ee, ah, oh, oo* are relatively easy to balance within your sections. There are, however, many other vocal sounds that can be misinterpreted. If you conduct choral music, it is important that you become familiar with the International Phonetic Alphabet, which has a specific symbol for each sound. Here is a list of some of the most important vocal sounds, and how they can be marked in a piece of music so everyone will pronounce them the same way.

PHONETIC SYMBOL	SOUND EXAMPLE	SCORE MARKING
i (long e)	see	ee
ɪ (short i)	king	ĭ
e (long a)	day	ay
ɛ (short e)	let	eh
æ (short a)	cat	ă
a	bath	à
ɑ	father	ah
ɒ (short o)	hot	ŏ
ɔ	talk	aw
o (long o)	low	oh
U	book	ŏo
u	who	oo
ɝ	earth	ur
ɚ	mother	er
ə	away	uh
ʌ (short u)	but	uh

Diphthongs

A *diphthong* is a compound vowel sound that combines two vowels and moves quickly from one to the other, creating a new sound. Diphthongs must be pronounced correctly by all of the members of your vocal ensemble if you are going to achieve a uniform sense of tone quality. If your chorus members fully understand the pronunciation of diphthongs and mark their scores in advance, you will have a more blended vocal quality, which will save you valuable rehearsal time.

PHONETIC SYMBOL	SOUND EXAMPLE	SCORE MARKING
aɪ	light	ah- ĭ
au	sound	ah-ŏo
ɔɪ	joy	aw-ĭ
eɪ	faith	ay-ĭ
ou	hope	oh-ŏo
ɪu	view	ĭ-ōo

The Left Hand

As a conductor, it is important that you learn to use the left hand effectively. Your right hand can be used to show tempo, character, dynamics, musical phrasing, and even cues, if they fit into the beat pattern easily; the left hand is used for cues that do not fit into the beat patterns, special emphasis of dynamics for specific sections of the ensemble, emphasis of special events in the music, sudden accents, *ppp* or *fff* markings, crescendos, diminuendos, and, of course, page turns.

It is important for your left hand to function independently from the right hand. This is not something that happens naturally but has to be trained. Too many conductors simply mirror the actions of the right hand with their left hand. This is not an effective use of your gestures.

You do not have to utilize the left hand all the time. When it is not in use, you can let it rest near your side in a relaxed position. Try to avoid leaving your hand near your stomach or in mid-air. It can become distracting and may confuse your performers.

As you train your left hand, remember to keep the fingers relaxed, but close together. This will give you better control and a better sound from your ensemble. Practice moving the left hand in long, smooth, slow motions without any bouncing or showing of the individual pulses. You will need to be able to move it independently, both vertically and horizontally, while the right hand beats standard patterns. These are some of the areas you can focus on for training and utilizing your left hand.

Accents and syncopations
Cues and cutoffs
Holds and releases
Phrasing and character
Crescendos and diminuendos
Sudden contrasts of dynamics
Gestures to adjust the balance

Accents and Syncopations

TYPES OF ACCENTS

An accent is *a musical notation that changes a note's articulation in a way that makes it slightly louder and more pronounced than the rest of the notes around it.* There are many ways to produce an accent and many ways that accents can be utilized in a musical passage.

Sometimes a composer uses an accent to start a musical motive so that it can clearly be heard. Other times, the accent might be used to bring out the main notes of the harmony, like an exclamation point. Most often, however, accents are used to draw attention to a specific rhythm or to create a contrasting inner rhythm in a phrase or musical section.

Tongued Accents

Woodwind and brass musicians play accents by adjusting the amount and the speed of the air they blow through their instruments, but the actual impact of the accent will be created by the motion of the tongue on the mouthpiece. Often, they will use syllables such as *ta* for horns and trumpets, and *doo* for the trombone, or *tu* for the tuba. Faster accents and articulations are produced by double-tonguing, using syllables such as *ti-ke, ti-ke-ti,* and *ti-ke-ti-ke.*

Bowed Accents

String players will create an accented sound by adjusting the weight, pressure, and speed of the bow as they begin the sound; the more weight and pressure, the heavier, or louder, the accent will be. A fast speed of the bow might project an accent quickly with short, sharp clarity, while a slower bow speed might achieve a louder, longer accent.

Struck Accents

Percussion instruments create accents by suddenly changing the weight and speed of the stroke, which will increase the articulation and volume of the accented note. They are not able to perform the same variety of accents as the winds or string instruments because it is impossible to control the sustained volume of their sound after the initial stroke.

Vocal Accents

Vocal accents are usually performed by emphasizing the consonant sounds and by increasing the volume of the note by using more breath. Words that start with an *explosive consonant* will always seem louder, even if an accent is not actually marked in the part. These consonants are *p, b, t, d, ch, j (dzh), k,* and *g.* For the articulation of these explosive consonants, the flow of the breath is stopped briefly, and the explosive sound results when the pressure of the breath is released. Letters like *s, sh,* and *z* also tend to cut through vocal texture, and it is important that the consonants on these syllables begin, and end, exactly together. Always keep the text in mind as you are evaluating the accents in a vocal piece.

NOTATION OF ACCENTS

In general, the most common marking for an accent is > but we also have accented articulations marked in the following ways.

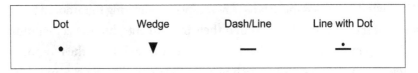

Dot	Wedge	Dash/Line	Line with Dot
•	▼	—	•/—

Each of these different types of accents will require you to show a different gesture to communicate the amount of stress, or articulation, the musician should use on that note. The different instruments will also require a slightly different gesture. Whenever you are conducting accents, you should give a noticeably shorter prep beat with a slight pause before the accented note. This will help the performers to begin the articulation together.

Accent gestures are always accompanied by a rebound motion. This rebound is necessary to show the release of the accented sound so that the musicians can end the accent together. The speed of the rebound off the attack will help to define the length of the actual accent.

After any accent is played, it is important for the ensemble to return to the main dynamic level and not remain at the louder dynamic level produced by the accent. Often groups perform louder and louder as they play through an accented passage of music. Returning to the original dynamic level is something that must be emphasized and practiced.

ACCENTED ENTRANCES

For all of the notated accents, there are different gestures that you can utilize to communicate the specific type of accented sound you would like to hear. Experiment with these motions listed below until you are comfortable with the various gestures. (See Video 4.9. ▶)

Volume Accents

Basic accent gestures can be shown at a variety of volume levels. Here are some examples for you to practice. Try performing these motions with either hand.

- Pop a balloon with a pin on the table in front of you (motion downward) (*piano*)
- Throw a marble at the table (*mezzo-piano*)
- Hold a small hammer in your right hand, raise it, then strike quickly downward and rebound after hitting the nail (*mezzo-forte*)
- Hold a large hammer in your right hand and hit a nail (*forte*)

Dots

The dot accent, or staccato articulation, is perhaps one of the easiest accents to show. It is done by a quick flick of the fingers, or the wrist. It can be conducted with energy toward the accent point, or energy away. Each motion will create a different type of accented attack.

- Flick drops of water off your fingertips or the tip of the baton (*downward—energy toward*)
- Pretend that you are touching a hot stove with your finger or the baton; feel your hand pull back quickly (*upward—energy away*)

Wedges

Musicians often have difficulty defining the sound difference between a standard dot accent and the wedge accent that Beethoven loved to use. The gesture for the wedge accent must convey more weight and force than the dot accent gesture.

- Hold a regular-size hammer; strike a large nail on the table in front of you and let your hand naturally rebound back up (*forte*)
- Hold a large maul in your hand; strike downward to pound in a stake, and let your hand naturally rebound (*fortissimo*)

Dashes

Musical dashes are communicated by using a pressing motion in the gesture. When a composer writes a "–" dash accent over a note, the musicians will sometimes overdo its length, playing it too long; or they will compensate in the opposite direction, playing the notes too separated. Depending upon how the dash is used in the phrase, you must make musical decisions regarding its length, and then show this length clearly with your gesture.

- Press down and then release the pressure on a wet sponge (*piano*)
- Press down and then release the pressure on a pillow (*mezzo-forte*)

Dots and Dashes Combined

The notation of a line dash on a note with an added dot is even more controversial. Does one play this short, or long? Which notation is dominant, the dot or the dash? Once you have made an artistic decision regarding the desired length of the note, you must show this exact length through your gesture. It is important for you to spend time developing the hand technique to accurately control the various lengths and volume levels of printed accents.

SYNCOPATION

Syncopations written within a musical phrase can create a feeling of accents. When you are conducting a syncopated passage, the syncopation always happens after a main beat. Because of this, you may instinctively want to insert extra "clicks" or subdivisions into the beat pattern to show the accent of the syncopation. This is wrong. Whenever you are conducting a syncopated passage, you must always conduct the strong beats, not the inner beats. Trust the musicians to play the syncopation rhythm as it is written. They simply need a clear pulse on the strong beats.

It is helpful when conducting syncopations to keep your general beat pattern small and clear. If the syncopated rhythm also contains written accents, give more accented motion to the main beats only. Never try to conduct the actual accents within the syncopated pattern.

When conducting syncopations, make sure that your beat gesture does not have a rebound. The rebound motion interferes with the players' ability to place the syncopated rhythm. Motions without a rebound might feel stiff, stopped, and unmusical to you; however, the clarity of this type of gesture is essential for musicians to play the inner beats of the pattern correctly. Here are some examples of syncopated rhythms for you to practice conducting.

OFFBEATS

Entrances or rhythmic patterns that come on an *offbeat* must be conducted in the same manner as a syncopated rhythm, even if it is only one note. Never emphasize the offbeat rhythm or entrance. Instead, give a very clear, accented main beat with no rebound, and allow the musician, or section, to place the offbeat entrance. This gesture is similar to chopping wood with a small hatchet. The hatchet strikes the wood and remains there; it does not bounce back up like the hammer. You have to wait a moment and then lift it up with a separate gesture. This motion works well for conducting offbeat patterns.

Cues and Cutoffs

CUES

One of the main jobs of the left hand is to motion to players, or singers, when it is time for them to begin. This is called *cuing*. When new instruments or vocal lines enter within the texture of a piece, it is important that the conductor give them a cue. The preparatory beat and breath before the cue is the most important item to communicate. The length and character of the preparatory breath signals the tone, tempo, and attack that you want the musicians to produce. The cue, like any preparatory beat, should always start *one full beat before the performers begin.* You do not have to cue every entrance, so the following is a list to help you decide whether an instrument, or section, needs a cue.

You should give a cue when:

- the instrument(s) or vocal line enters for the first time
- musicians enter after a long rest
- musicians have an important melodic or harmonic line
- there is a tricky rhythm involved with the entrance
- you want to encourage the performer, and also control the quality and character of the sound

- you need to communicate a sudden change of dynamics
- the melody is passed from one instrument or line to another, as in a fugue
- the part is difficult because of extremes of the range (either low or high)

You will also want to cue

- isolated pizzicato notes in the strings, or isolated chords
- special percussion effects such as cymbals, triangle, woodblock, or gong

Types of Cues

When we think of the cuing motion, we usually think of cuing with the left hand, but there are additional ways to give a cue to an instrument or section.

Left-hand cue—This is the most common type of cue and it is usually performed using the fingertips, or with the first finger lightly touching the thumb.

Open-hand cue—This gesture is also performed by the left hand, but with the palm up. You can use this motion to show a legato entrance in order to inspire a beautiful melodic line.

Baton cue—If your left hand is already busy showing dynamics, you might give a cue by pointing the tip of your baton at a player or section.

Head cue—If you do not want to disrupt the flow of the phrase with a large hand cue, and if the cue is an acknowledgment to the player to confirm that they are in the right place, you might give a cue with a slight nod of the head.

Eye cue—Eye cues are an extension of head cues, but they are usually done in advance by establishing eye contact with a player who has not been playing for a long time. It is important to catch the player's eye so that he or she can prepare for the entrance.

How to Cue

To cue with your left hand, you will use a small motion with your first finger lightly touching your thumb. Your palm will be basically pointed outward. The cuing motion is similar to tapping once on a door, placing dabs of paint on a canvas, or putting a thumbtack in a wall. The size and force of the gesture is directly related to the volume you want to convey.

Be sure to give only one specific type of cue at a time. If you are giving a left-hand cue, do not give a head cue at the same time. Giving both sends a mixed message. There should be no extraneous motion of the head and chin while cuing, unless you are specifically giving a head cue.

As you practice cuing, remember that *the preparatory breath and gesture are always given one full beat ahead of the cue*, as in an entrance beat. This is the motion that encourages performers to breathe in the correct tempo. It is also important to establish eye contact with the individual, or section, a few bars before the entrance, to make sure that they are not lost and that they are ready to play or sing. Your cue motion should be directed specifically to the person, or group of people, making the entrance, not a random motion in the air. Do not let your attention leave the performer until you are sure that he or she has entered and is playing everything correctly. This includes listening to and adjusting the articulation, and also listening for tone color and balance with the other musicians.

Cues on the Beat

When giving a cue that occurs on a strong beat, it is important to show a good breath. The cue motion is similar to pulling a dart out of the board with your fingers as you are inhaling; and then throwing it back at the board with a release. The gesture is small, and your hand should only move about four to five inches. The moment of connection to the dart establishes the beginning of the preparatory beat, which connects you to your musicians. The thrown release of the dart is the cue gesture with a rebound. If the music is more legato in character, you can use a gesture that has more of a press-and-release motion and less ictus.

Cues Off the Beat

To conduct cues that begin on an offbeat, it is necessary to use a gesture similar to the "dart cue" gesture, but instead of a dart, imagine you are holding a small spring at the end of your finger. Move your hand forward and bounce the spring off the wall in front of you on the strong beat before the offbeat entrance. Do not try to show any additional inner pulse on the offbeat; just feel the bounce of the spring. The musicians will place their entrance on the offbeat, as long as you show the rebound and you do not stop the motion of your hand.

Multiple Cues on Different Beats

To practice showing many cues in a row, write the words "1 *and* 2 *and* 3 *and* 4" over and over again on a piece of paper. Now circle a number or "*and*" from within each grouping of four. Do not circle the same thing for each bar. The circled number or word will represent the cues you are going to show. Now, as you conduct a four pattern with your right hand, show the cue entrances with your left hand for each of your circled items. After practicing this, make a new number chart and try cuing with your left hand while beating patterns of three, five, and six.

Cue Motions

A variety of gestures can be useful to communicate different types of cues. Here are a few. (See Video 4.10. ▶)

- Pulling a dart out of a dart board and throwing it
  For clear articulated entrances

- Bouncing a small spring on a wall in front of you
  For lifted, lighter entrances

- Pulling a slingshot back and releasing it
  For loud, but short, accented cues

- Pressing and holding a buzzer
  For cues of longer, sustained notes

- Brushing your hand across a table (with the palm sideways)
  *For legato cues involving many players performing a softer
  dynamic*

- Throwing a Frisbee with your left hand
  A cue for showing the expansiveness of the phrase

When Not to Cue

In some specific circumstances you should not try to cue. This is true when the entrances come very quickly in a thick contrapuntal texture. Too many cues that are too close together are confusing to the performers, as they might not be sure whom you are indicating. You will also look a little silly pointing all over the place that quickly. It is best to insist that the members of your ensemble count carefully during these types of passages, and for you to trust their individual musicianship.

Cuing Patterns and Diagrams

If you have a fugal section that does require the cuing of multiple instruments one after the other, it is best if you make a cuing diagram and memorize the pattern of your gestures. Make a list of the instruments you are cuing in the order that they play, and memorize it. This will help you feel more secure when you are conducting this section of the piece. You need to train not only your mind regarding the order of the cues, but also your hands so that you master the physical motions. If you experience difficulty cuing different sections in a fast tempo, practice the cuing pattern slowly until your hands are familiar with the movements. Once the pattern is memorized, you can practice it anywhere, mentally seeing it and also physically practicing the motions.

Sample Patterns

Strings

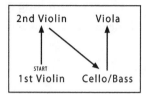 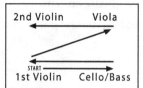 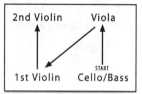

Woodwinds

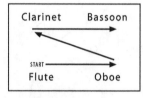 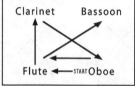 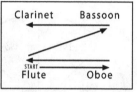

Chorus

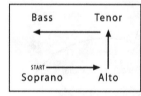 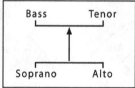 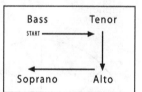

Cues with Different Seating Setups

Sometimes you may walk into a rehearsal where you are guest conducting, and the group will be set up differently from what you were expecting. It is important to anticipate this situation and to practice your cuing patterns using different ensemble stage setups. If you have memorized the order of the instrument entrances, it is relatively easy to retrain your hands to cue in different places. Practice the cuing exercises above, but use a variety of seating setups.

Make a list of random instruments to cue in the order that you wrote them down. From the charts below, select a different string setup to use with each full orchestra diagram and practice giving these cues. Then experiment with showing cues using the different band setups. Write a list of vocal cues and practice with the chorus diagrams. Observe how long it takes you to retrain your hands for the placement of the gestures for each new diagram.

Possible String Seating

Standard

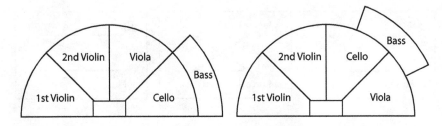

Antiphonal

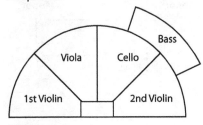
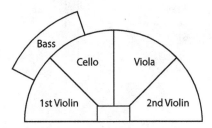

Full Orchestra

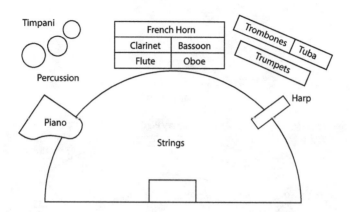

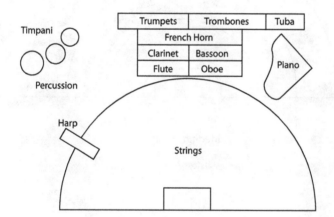

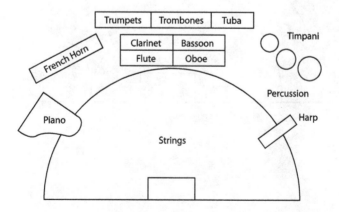

Large Band

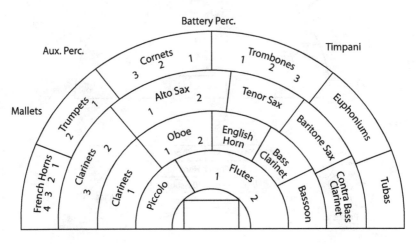

Medium Band

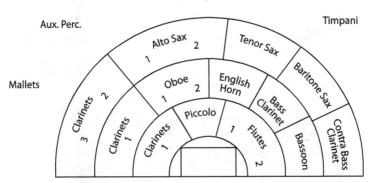

Chorus

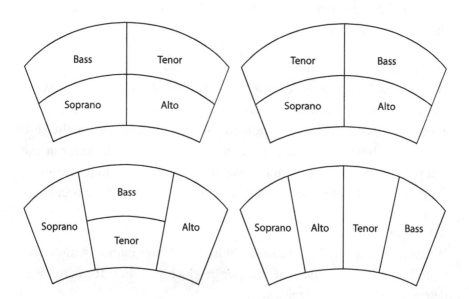

CUTOFFS

Every cutoff requires a preparatory motion, or breath, to alert the ensemble. This motion must communicate the specific type of release desired. Do you want a sound that stops abruptly, or do you want the sound to be lifted and ringing? If you are working with a chorus, what is the exact syllable of the cutoff, and on which beat, or part of the beat, do you want it placed?

Cutoffs

- Up-and-Down
- Backward "e"
- Dead Stop Cutoff
- Lifted Cutoff

Video 4.11

A cutoff can be given with either hand, depending on the musical context. Cutoffs can be shown with a short, up-and-down, ictus motion that releases the sound with a rebound off the beat; or with a small, circular motion, like a backward letter "e."

Up-and-Down Cutoffs

To practice cutoffs using the up-and-down motion, place your hand, or baton, on your table of sound. This is the position for your hand when holding a note before the cutoff. Now, lift your hand up about two inches and then tap your fingertips, or the tip of your baton, gently on your table of sound, letting it rebound up. The first lift is the preparatory beat, and the tap on the table is the exact point of the cutoff.

Backward Letter "e" Cutoffs

With the backward letter "e" cutoff, the top part of the circle is your preparatory breath and motion for the cutoff, and the end of "e" gesture is the exact cutoff point. If you are conducting with your hand, you might close your hand slightly and touch your thumb to your middle finger at the end point of the "e" to show the cutoff of the sound. Your movement will continue slightly after your hand has closed and the cutoff has occurred.

Release of Sound

When ending a cutoff, you can use either an abrupt motion with no rebound, or a lifted release. The manner in which you show the cutoff will determine the release of the last note.

> **Dead Stop Cutoff**—This motion stops completely on the exact cutoff. The gesture is similar to turning off a light switch. There is no rebound or motion after the moment of the cutoff.
>
> **Lifted Cutoff**—This cutoff motion uses a rebound and you will actually lift the sound, and allow the sound to continue to ring after the core of the note has stopped.

Multiple Cutoffs Exercise

With your piece of paper and numbers, do the same type of exercise as the multiple cuing exercise, but instead of cuing, give the motion of a cutoff on each of the circled numbers or words. Practice showing the difference between a stopped cutoff and a lifted cutoff. Experiment with making your motions larger and smaller depending on the number of people involved. See the difference in cutting off just one player and cutting off an entire section. If you are showing a cutoff for only part of your ensemble, be sure that you are encouraging the others to continue at the same time. You can do this by showing a smooth and continuous beat pattern with your right hand as you are showing the cutoff gesture with your left hand, or by holding your hand still to sustain a chord or note after the cutoff gesture is given.

Lifts, Holds, Rests, and Releases

LIFTS AND CAESURAS

A *lift*, or a *caesura*, is a pause that occurs between two notes, or immediately before the beginning of the next bar or section. This pause is caused by a stop, or lift, of the sound. If a cutoff is involved, it will need a rebound motion. Sometimes you will be required to insert an extra preparatory beat after the lift, or caesura, in order to prepare for the next entrance.

There are three basic types of lifts or caesuras:

- A short pause in the motion of the music indicated by a ' or //, over the bar
- A short breath, or lift, to show a fresh beginning between two distinct phrases
- A complete break that is used to separate musical sections of different characters

RESTS

A *rest* is a suspension of the regular pulse of the piece. Most of the time, rests are conducted with a dead-beat gesture, or a motion that does not have energy or breath. It is important that these silent beats do not have any rebound and that they are very small and inactive in character.

Rests that are written at the beginning of a piece, even when no one plays, must be clearly shown so that those counting will not lose their places. Rests written at the end of a piece, when no one is playing, do not have to be beaten.

Rests are conducted by placing or moving your hand on your table of sound without any energy using a dead-beat gesture. Conduct the following example utilizing dead-beat gestures for the rests and active beat gestures for the notes. Make sure each entrance is preceded by a clear preparatory beat and breath. (See Video 4.12. ▶)

ACCOMPANIMENT RESTS AND RECITATIVE

When a part contains passages in which musicians are resting for a long time, such as solo sections in a concerto, you must clearly show the downbeats of these bars of rest, but you do not have to show all the beats in the bar if the tempo is steady and the music predictable. Trust that your musicians know how to count. They will, however, depend on you to give them a signal before their next entrance, and a good breath and cue. If you are not clear with these cues, your musicians might come in late or miss the entrance completely.

If you are conducting opera recitative, there are two commonly used approaches. The first involves moving the baton slowly in tempo with dead-beat gestures throughout all the rests until the next entrance occurs. If it is a short recitative, you can show each beat of the bar with minimal motion. If it is a longer section, you might want to use a single beat to mark each bar as it occurs, and then not beat the rest of the pulses in each bar.

The second approach to conducting recitative involves quickly showing passive downbeats equal to the total number of bars of rest in the recitative before the next entrance, and then waiting with your baton in position to cue the next entrance. The waiting position is one full beat before the entrance of the ensemble. When the singer or instrumentalist reaches that point, give a strong preparatory beat and breath to bring everyone in.

In opera recitative, if the entrance note is on the beat, you would give a standard preparatory beat, one full beat before the entrance. If the entrance occurs after the beat, or on an offbeat, you would use a gesture of syncopation—a motion that shows a strong impact and then stops.

It is useful to mark your score so that you know on which beat you must wait to be in position for the next cue. Here are sample symbol markings for your score. (See Video 4.13. ▶)

Symbols

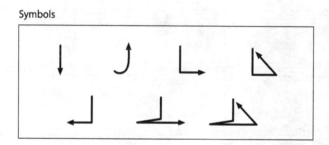

Recitative: **Thus Saith the Lord**
Handel - Messiah

When you are conducting recitative, be sure to study the soloist's words and music so that you can be flexible in following them. You should memorize key words that align with ensemble entrances and clearly mark these words in your score.

If you are holding chords underneath a vocal recitative where the chords are played softly, but with sustained energy, it is important that you communicate continuous energy and that you do not relax the musical intensity as you hold these notes. Even if the same chord, or

note, is held continuously for many measures, the first beat of each
bar must be clearly marked for the musicians who are counting rests.
While holding these notes or chords, make sure that your baton fin-
ishes and holds in the right position to show the breath for the next
musical entrance.

FERMATAS

A *fermata* is a musical notation that is used to extend a note, chord, or
moment of silence in the music. The length of the fermata must be *longer
than the normal value of the note or rest that it is placed on*, however the
exact length is not specified. It is up to the conductor to define the proper
length of each fermata.

In some musical style periods, it is common to hold a fermata for
double the value of the original length of the note. This formula can work
but should not be taken as the solution for all fermatas. You must use your
own musicality to determine the length that sounds correct and will sustain the momentum and energy of the composition.

When you conduct fermatas, you must plan where your baton will be
at the end of the hold so that it is in the proper position to prepare the next
entrance. You must identify the beat on which the next sound begins, and
then back up at least one full beat so that you can give the right preparatory gesture. Sometimes, when holding a fermata, it is necessary to add an
extra beat into the pattern, repeating the beat you are holding, in order to
conduct the preparatory beat for the next entrance.

TYPES OF FERMATAS

All fermatas fall into two basic categories: (1) fermatas that are held and continue without a pause; and (2) fermatas that need a cutoff. Within the latter category there are two subtypes of fermatas that use a cutoff: (1) fermatas where the cutoff becomes the preparatory beat for the next entrance; and (2) fermatas that require a full cutoff followed by a pause. After the pause, a new preparatory beat is given to show the next entrance.

> **Fermatas**
>
> - Continuous Fermatas
> - Fermatas with Cutoffs
> - Fermatas under Cadenzas
> - Re-Beaten Fermatas
>
> **Video 4.14**

Continuous Fermatas

A continuous fermata needs no cutoff of the sound, and the held note continues into the next phrase without a pause. With this type of fermata, the right hand stops on the fermata note and holds it. As you are holding the fermata, you can support the sound showing a crescendo or diminuendo as desired with your left hand. At the end of the fermata, there is no rest after the hold. As the note is still being held, your right hand should begin to move to show the preparatory beat for the next note, and then this gesture continues into the next beat.

Scheherazade - movement 2, m.367-m.373
Rimsky-Korsakov

Fermatas with Cutoffs

Fermatas with cutoffs begin in the same manner as the continuous fermata. The right hand stops beating to sustain the hold for the fermata, while the left hand is used to control the dynamic levels. In this case, though, the left hand is then used to show a cutoff, while the right hand gets ready to show the new preparatory beat.

Two types of fermatas use cutoffs:

- *A fermata with a short silence that is up to one beat or less in length and then the piece continues.* When you are conducting this type of fermata, the cutoff gesture can also be the preparation gesture for the next entrance. The cutoff creates a slight pause after the fermata. This pause is usually the length of the preparatory beat.

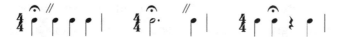

- *A fermata followed by a silence or rest considerably longer than one beat.* When this is the case, two separate gestures must be given: one gesture for the cutoff, and the other gesture to show the preparatory beat for the next entrance.

Fermatas under Cadenzas

When you conduct a fermata under a cadenza passage, your right hand will continue to show the extended hold while the left hand is used to cue in any musicians who might have separate entrances within that hold.

Scheherazade - movement 2, m.164
Rimsky-Korsakov

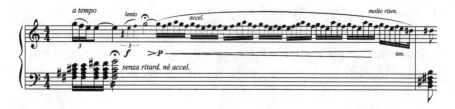

Scheherazade - movement 2, m.108-m.109
Rimsky-Korsakov

RE-BEATEN FERMATAS

There are also situations when a fermata occurs on a specific beat and the next entrance begins just one beat later. For the musicians to know when to play, or sing, after the fermata, you will need to show the beat you are holding twice. You will arrive on the fermata note for the hold, and then show it again with a breath as the preparatory beat for the next note.

If you are in a one-beat pattern, like a fast 3/8 or 3/4, this re-beating will involve showing an extra bar as your preparatory beat for the next entrance.

GENERAL RULES FOR FERMATAS

When you are holding a fermata, make sure that you gradually move your hand to the necessary position to show the preparatory beat for the next entrance.

Sometimes the music after a fermata is in a new tempo, such as an *allegro* after a slow introduction. Make sure that your preparatory beat is clearly in the new tempo.

If a fermata occurs on the last beat of a measure, keep any rebound motion low so that your hand has room to give the new preparatory beat.

If a situation arises where different musical lines have fermatas of varying note values, you can cut off the group that has the shorter value with your left hand while you continue to hold the others with your right hand.

If a fermata is placed over a long note or rest, there are situations where you should continue to beat through the held note, or silence, within the pattern until the final count is finished. Beating through to the end note value will help avoid confusion regarding which beat you are holding. These beats should be shown as "dead" beats without energy or rebound, but if performers are playing or singing through this fermata, you must still maintain an overall sense of energy.

Once you are comfortable with showing the different types of fermatas, you can then focus on gestures for changing and controlling tempo and dynamics.

Controlling Tempo and Volume

GOING FASTER AND SLOWER

Perhaps you remember that first experience when you discovered that if you moved your arms faster the group would actually follow you, and if you slowed down your gestures, the group would slow down. Being able to control the tempo of a piece of music is essential to creating the musical interpretation. This is something you must master to be an effective conductor.

Selecting the Tempo

One of the most important tasks of a conductor is to establish the tempo for a piece of music. With each composition, there is a certain tempo that feels right and works musically. How do you find the right tempo?

Most new scores contain metronome markings by the composer printed in the music. With your metronome, check the printed tempo marking against the contour of the music. Does it make sense? Does the music flow smoothly? Now, find the most intricate passage in the movement or piece. How does that passage sound at this tempo? Does the tempo still seem right, or does it need to be adjusted? With all pieces, the most involved passage, and also the passage with the least motion, must be checked to make sure both work within the selected tempo.

If the composer did not mark any tempo indications in the music, try singing the melodies of the piece. At what tempo can you sing the phrases in one breath? Test that on the fastest and slowest passages and see if you can find the tempo that fits for everything. Once you have decided on what is appropriate for the piece, make sure that you notate your tempo marking clearly in your score so that every time you rehearse the piece, you are conducting the same tempo.

Tempo Terminology

When composers have not marked specific metronome instructions in the score, they usually have written some musically descriptive terms to point you in the right direction. This is particularly common with any music written before Beethoven, but it is also prevalent with scores by Gustav Mahler and other more recent composers. Words like *allegro, adagio,* or *presto* are often used to describe the general feeling or mood the composer wishes to convey. Still, it is up to you as the conductor to decide which specific tempo is right for a piece to bring it to life.

Other Considerations

The size of the ensemble and the dimensions of the rehearsal room or concert hall will also influence your decisions regarding tempo. Smaller ensembles can play faster and maintain a clearer sound than large ensembles. Rooms with less echo will allow you to play certain passages faster, while a room with significant reverberation will quickly muddy the quality of the sound. This might require you to slow your tempos slightly to maintain clarity. Performing spaces that allow the players to hear each other well will increase the ensemble's ability to play difficult, fast passages together.

Showing the Right Tempo

Knowing the correct tempo and actually communicating it to a group of musicians are different matters. You will set your tempo with your upbeat, or a preparatory beat, but tempo is rarely consistent throughout an entire piece or movement. You must be able to beat evenly but also be able to show subtle changes in tempo that might occur in the middle of a bar on beats other than one.

When establishing the tempo for a piece of music, the speed of your motions is always related to the size of the gesture. Small gestures can be performed quickly while larger gestures require more time to travel between beats. As you set your tempo, gauge the size of your gesture relative to the tempo that you are trying to communicate. In general, the following applies:

Fast Tempos	To communicate a fast tempo, keep the beat small with a clear ictus. A large beat tends to be unclear in a fast tempo.
Slow Tempos	To show a slow tempo, you can use a larger beat, but you must also learn to control the movements of your hands so they are able to move smoothly, without jerking or stopping. It is important to constantly feel the resistance of perceived weight within the beat of a slow tempo.

AVOID CONDUCTING SUBDIVISIONS

Even though you may be tempted to subdivide your beat pattern in a very slow tempo, it is not a good idea unless the music absolutely requires it. Always strive to conduct in the larger beat pattern, and develop your technique so that you can control and sustain very slow motions with your hand. As you practice slow gestures, continually subdivide each beat in your mind so that you connect to the inner pulse. If you do not subdivide each beat, you may rush your pattern. Conducting in a large beat pattern will produce a freer and more relaxed sound that allows the music to "breathe." This is clearer for the musicians to follow because you trust them and are out of their way.

ESTABLISHING INNER RHYTHM

As a conductor, you must have a strong, ingrained sense of rhythm. It is also essential to develop the habit of hearing the inner 16th-note values, not just the quarter-note and half-note subdivisions within a musical phrase. For any passage with intricate rhythms, it is important to keep your ears focused on the fastest moving line. The players performing

16th- and 32nd-notes must have time to place all of their notes within the bar. If the other parts rush, and you follow them because you are not subdividing carefully, you may find that you have a musical train wreck on your hands.

It is helpful to set your metronome to click out the inner beats of your tempo while you are practicing. This will make it easier for you to develop an internal sense of subdivision. As you are conducting long notes in the music, focus on the inner subdivision beats of these long notes in your head. This will keep you from conducting inconsistently in the name of "musicality," and it will allow the ensemble to play better together.

DRAGGING OR RUSHING

When an ensemble is playing at a tempo different from the one you desire, you are probably causing this conflict through something you are doing. Perhaps you rushed your preparatory beat by not subdividing carefully; or perhaps an extra click shown with your wrist or elbow resulted in the ensemble playing slightly slower. The first thing you must do when the group is not playing together is to evaluate what you are doing that may be confusing. Try beating smaller and clearer to make sure that you are sending only one message to the musicians. If the problem with the tempo is from the beginning of the piece or a section you just began, try starting again, but this time, give two preparatory beats before you start. Often in fast tempos, a single preparatory beat is not enough to clearly establish the tempo.

Dragging

When you hear that the ensemble is consistently dragging, or playing slower than your beat, you are probably beating too large and showing too much rebound. Changing the size of your beat to a smaller pattern with less rebound will probably solve the problem. A large rebound creates a space in time during which you cannot accurately control the sound of the ensemble. With a more fluid, connected beat, you will have a better chance of pulling the group forward so that they cannot slow down.

Dragging often occurs when you are too focused on the main beats and you are waiting to hear the sound before continuing. Instead, concentrate more on thinking the subdivided inner pulses between the beats, not the main beats. These inner subdivisions provide the preparation signal that defines the tempo for the main beats. Always move forward toward the next subdivision. You can also use a circular motion to bring the group back into tempo. This can be shown by your left hand while your right hand is giving the main pulse. This gesture is interpreted immediately by musicians to mean that they are behind and need to go faster.

Rushing

If the ensemble is rushing, which they will often do when they are sight-reading pieces with difficult 16th- or 32nd- notes, you should first beat smaller to get their attention. Once you are sure you have their focus, you can gradually make your beat pattern larger, pulling the tempo back slightly to control the rushing. As you do this, emphasize the main beats with a more marked gesture, but still keep your rebound small so that you do not lose control of the sound.

Changing Your Tempo

If players are to follow you, they must sense what you are going to do before you do it. They cannot just follow; they must also be able to anticipate. The tempo is established by communicating a very clear preparatory beat. Sections of music that require a new tempo must be treated exactly as if they were the beginning of a new piece. It is helpful to make the preparatory beat for each new tempo slightly larger than you would normally conduct. As you do this, though, make sure that this increase in size does not slow your beat pattern. A larger preparatory motion gives the players a clearer signal to follow as they try to anticipate your new tempo.

When you are moving from a slower tempo to a faster tempo, as in an "Introduction and Allegro" section of a piece, it is important for your beat pattern to remain low and for you not to use a rebound motion as you end the slow section. This will enable your hand to be in the right position to introduce the new preparatory beat that will set the new tempo. You may have to stop beating for a moment before giving the new preparatory beat for the *allegro* tempo.

TEMPO CHANGE WITHOUT TIME FOR PREP

Sometimes a very sudden tempo change will occur in a piece when there is no time to give a proper preparatory beat. When this happens, you must stop conducting in the old tempo slightly early, and while the ensemble continues playing the last few notes in the previous tempo, you quickly give a small, new preparatory beat in the new tempo. Make sure that the first few beats of the new tempo are conducted with a larger beat pattern that is very clear and marked. You have to convey your conviction of the new tempo with great confidence when a tempo change occurs suddenly.

CHANGES OF TIME SIGNATURE WITHOUT CHANGE OF TEMPO

When a composer writes a time signature change but keeps the inner pulse of the music the same, the audience may hear it as a tempo change because of the shift in rhythm. It is very common to see ♩ = ♩ or ♪ = ♪ notated in a score. As you conduct these types of transitions, you must maintain the same exact pulse even though your beat pattern may be changing dramatically.

TEMPO RELATIONSHIPS

Often, a previously established tempo has a direct relationship to a new tempo in a piece. In this situation, the music might be notated twice as fast, *doppio movimento* ♩ = ♩ or twice as slow, ♩ = ♩. To keep the pulse relationship consistent, you must focus on the strong pulses and keep the relationship the same.

Sometimes a tempo change occurs in which there is a metronomic relationship, but it is not an equal one. Perhaps one eighth-note (♪) of a quarter note triplet (♩♩♩) in the first tempo equals a standard eighth note in the new tempo. For most music written before 1900, the musical transitions make more sense if you can establish a tempo relationship between the two sections, even when this relationship is not specifically noted by the composer. This also applies to the relationship between the movements of a piece. Everything will flow more effectively if there is a metronomic relationship between all the tempos you have selected.

Of course, there are situations involving tempo changes in which absolutely no pulse relationship exists. These are the most difficult to conduct. You must be secure with the tempos of each individual section, especially if you are starting and stopping and working the two sections separately during a rehearsal. It is essential for the technical proficiency of the performers that the music be rehearsed at the same tempo selected for the performance, except for when you might be rehearsing a technically difficult passage slowly. To keep your tempos consistent, carefully notate the metronome markings at the beginning of each section in your score and have your metronome handy during rehearsals to check your tempos.

Pacing Your Tempo Change

As you are conducting, it may be necessary to adjust a tempo slightly faster or slower in order to create a smooth transition between two different tempos. To make a transition sound seamless, define the beginning and ending tempo, then calculate the number of beats needed to make the change and distribute the basic metronome markings between these two tempos. You should identify a precise metronome marking for each bar to help you systematically move toward the new tempo. A dial metronome is very useful for practicing accelerandos and rallentandos because you can turn it one click at a time, either faster or slower, to establish a uniform pacing. It is helpful to write these metronome notations on your score above each bar to remind you of how you will shape these tempo changes.

Accelerando

To conduct an accelerando, you must carefully listen to the ensemble, making sure you catch their attention with your eyes and hands before trying to move them forward. It is important that you do not try to change the tempo until you have their full attention. Therefore, you must prepare for the tempo change a few bars in advance of the point the accelerando occurs in the music.

As you start the accelerando, you will need to reduce the rebound of your beat and the amount of space between the beats. Focus on emphasizing the core beats as you make the accelerando. Plan the pacing and practice it with a metronome so that your accelerando is even and moves forward in a steady manner. As the tempo increases, your beat motion should become smaller. Here are some general guidelines for conducting an accelerando. (See Video 5.1. ▶)

If you want to go faster:

- Use a more vertical gesture
- Beat smaller and make the distance between the beats gradually smaller

- Increase the speed of the movement between your beats
- Focus on the core beats and emphasize them with a dry staccato feel
- Utilize a circular type beat to move the group forward

Exercises:

- Conduct basic eighth notes in a four pattern. Start at ♪ = 60, then gradually accelerate to ♩ = 140. Start by showing the accelerando over eight bars. Notate the tempo you need to conduct at each bar in order to make the change seem gradual.

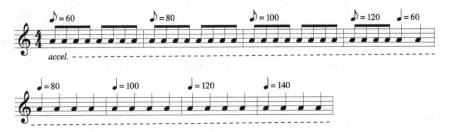

- Now, practice the same exercise again, only reduce the number of bars used for the accelerando. Make sure you write down the metronome arrival point for each bar.
- Practice repeating this exercise, reducing the number of bars each time, until you can conduct an accelerando within a single bar.

Merged Beats

As you make an accelerando from a slow tempo to a faster tempo, it may be necessary for you to *merge* your beats. Merged beats gradually become less defined to enable you to shift from one type of beat pattern to another. (See Video 5.2. ▶)

Exercises:

- To make an accelerando from a subdivided four pattern into a normal four pattern, start by conducting slowly a subdivided four pattern. In the next bar, gradually round out your "*and*" beats until you are conducting smoothly without showing the subdivision.

Then, as you continue, slowly reduce the size of your overall gesture and increase the tempo.

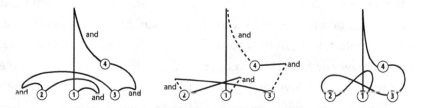

- To move from a four pattern to a two pattern within an accelerando, you must gradually stop showing the second and third
  beats. First, make them smaller with very little motion to either
  side, then, move into a subdivided two-beat gesture while still
  showing all four pulses. Gradually round out your motion into a
  curved two-beat pattern as you increase the tempo.

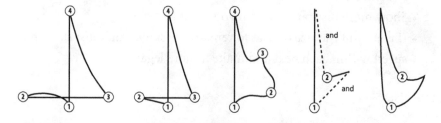

- To conduct an accelerando going from a three-beat pattern to a
  one-beat pattern, first conduct a few bars in the three-beat pattern. Then, gradually make the second beat smaller and closer to
  your first beat. As you increase the tempo, merge your gesture by
  rounding the second beat. Eventually, you will conduct a straight
  line downward, followed by a curved gesture upward. The individual second and third beats disappear from the gesture, but you
  must still count them internally.

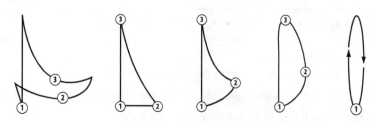

RALLENTANDO

In your conducting, you will encounter many situations when you must control a rallentando or ritard. Sometimes it is helpful to use your left hand to focus attention before you start a rallentando. Make sure to establish good eye contact, and carefully plan out the pacing of each tempo change. Once you have the full attention of your ensemble, gradually enlarge the size of your beat and slow down the speed and amount of rebound between beats. The result will be a more legato, connected gesture, with an emphasis on stretching the energy between beats to gradually slow the tempo. Here are the general rules for conducting rallentandos. (See Video 5.3. ▶)

If you want to go slower:

- Use a more horizontal gesture
- Slow the speed of your rebound gesture
- Beat larger and gradually expand the distance between the beats
- Show more resistance within your beat pattern
- If you want the size of beat to remain the same, you must slow the speed within each beat and make it more legato.

Exercises:

- Repeat the exercises that you used to practice an accelerando, only reverse the process. Start by conducting repeated eighth notes in a four pattern at a tempo of ♩ = 140, and then slow down to ♪ = 60 over an eight-bar phrase.

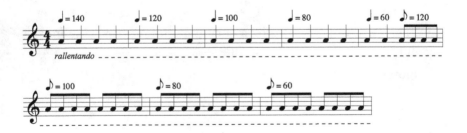

- Now, perform the same exercise using gradually fewer bars to make the tempo change. Mark the metronome counts in your score at each bar to help you pace the ritard.

Conducting Subdivisions

Sometimes, to slow down a tempo or make a large rallentando, you have to go into a subdivided beat to control the sound because it is difficult to maintain a larger beat pattern when the basic pulse goes below 50 on the metronome. Therefore, as the tempo slows, you will need to start conducting the inner beats. A subdivided beat provides a sturdier motion and can facilitate rhythms, accents, or entrances in a slow tempo. Once you have begun subdividing a beat pattern, you should continue the subdivision until the tempo moves faster again. Resist the temptation to alternate back and forth between subdivided and non-subdivided beat patterns as this is confusing for your ensemble. (See Video 5.4. ▶)

Exercises:

- To practice conducting a subdivided beat with a *stop-lift* gesture, place your hand on your table of sound, then lift it up and place it to your left where the second beat would be; lift again and place your hand where the third beat would be; then lift and place the fourth beat. Each time you place your hand, you are showing the strong beat. When you lift your hand, you are showing the *and* or the subdivision of the main beat. Practice moving from a connected beat pattern to this stop-start, subdivided type of beat pattern.
- To move from a four pattern into a subdivided four pattern, you must begin to stop your gesture on each beat, then lift upward to show the *and* beat, or subdivision. Gradually round out your gesture until you are conducting a subdivided four pattern.

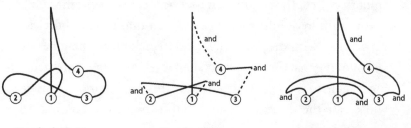

Standard 4 Pattern   Stop-beat Pattern   Subdivided 4 Pattern

- To practice moving from a three pattern to a subdivided three pattern, you will follow the same technique as in the exercise above, gradually stopping and lifting the beat, and then rounding out the gesture to show the clear subdivisions.

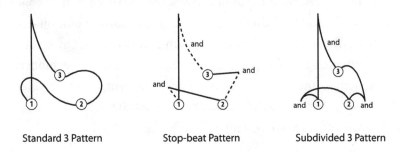

Standard 3 Pattern   Stop-beat Pattern   Subdivided 3 Pattern

- Experiment with shifting from a regular two-beat pattern to a subdivided two pattern. Visualize touching the table, lifting your hand, and then putting it back on the table and lifting again.

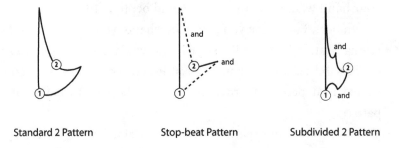

Standard 2 Pattern   Stop-beat Pattern   Subdivided 2 Pattern

- For a subdivision in one, instead of one continuous circular motion, imagine picking up peas, or plucking a chicken. Beat one is the point where you move downward to connect with the imaginary object. The subdivided beat occurs on the lift motion.
- If you want to divide a one-beat motion into three subdivisions, experiment with dropping the hand to pick up an imaginary object, moving that object to your shelf level, stopping, and then lifting it again to your starting position. This combination of motions will create the three separate impulses needed to communicate three inner beats.

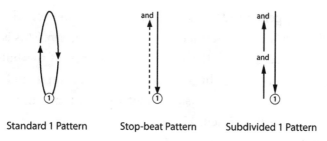

Standard 1 Pattern   Stop-beat Pattern   Subdivided 1 Pattern

- If you want to expand your beats during a rallentando from a one-beat pattern to a three-beat pattern, follow the diagram below.

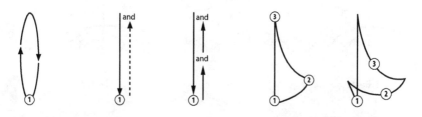

Second and Third Rebound

To conduct in an extremely slow tempo, or for pieces in a slow 6/8, 9/8, or 12/8, you can gradually shift to a type of beat that utilizes two rebound motions, creating a triple subdivision. Imagine that you are bouncing a small ball. Bounce it on the floor and it will bounce again on its own, only not as high and with less energy on the second and third bounce. For a triple subdivision, we show these additional bouncing gestures slightly to the side of the main beat.

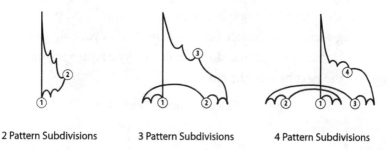

2 Pattern Subdivisions   3 Pattern Subdivisions   4 Pattern Subdivisions

Conducting Individual Beats

For the slowest tempos, you must essentially conduct each inner pulse as if it were a main beat. Therefore, every stroke is equally marked, and your pattern is no longer considered a subdivided pattern but actually becomes an eight pattern, a nine pattern, or even a twelve pattern. This is reserved for very slow pieces where the music calls for each of the pulses to be shown individually. With this type of conducting, you would place the beats in the same manner as a subdivided beat pattern, but the gestures are larger and more defined. Here are some diagrams for conducting patterns of 8, 9, and 12. (See Video 5.5. ▶)

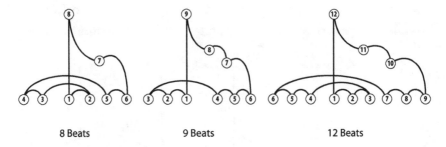

| 8 Beats | 9 Beats | 12 Beats |

Subdividing a Single Beat

When you are conducting subtle rubato, or small ritards, it is necessary to master the technique of subdividing a single beat. To do this, you must remain connected to the inner energy within the beat so you can gently expand it. An arc gesture can be useful for showing the subdivisions of a single beat within a ritard. This inner ritard can happen within any beat of the bar. A single rubato beat can be divided into two or three inner subdivisions, depending upon the demands of the music and how much you want to slow down. Practice conducting these gestures in the air to show a clear subdivision of a single beat within a standard beat pattern. When conducting a ritard on a single beat, each motion of your subdivided beat should be gradually larger and slower, followed by a return to your original tempo on the next beat of the bar.

Two Inner Subdivisions of a Single Beat

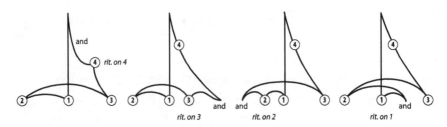

Three Inner Subdivisions of a Single Beat

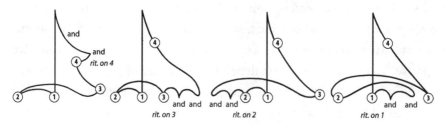

SHAPING DYNAMICS

Musical expression relies on the variety of the color and volume of the sound that you are able to illicit from your musicians through your gestures. Even though dynamic levels are notated on the music of each performer, your conducting gestures need to show and reinforce these dynamics.

Music written before 1850 tended to utilize uniform dynamics for all the instruments or voices. With music of this era, even though the dynamics are marked the same, you should encourage players to scale their dynamics according to the musical importance of their part. The melody should be played at the loudest volume, and a countermelody at a lesser level. The bass part that provides the harmonic structure is always an important musical line to bring out. Held notes that are a part of the inner harmony, or short harmonic punctuations played by instruments such as trumpets and the timpani, should be played at a softer volume level, even though their dynamic marking on the page might be the same as that for the other instruments.

From around 1850 onward, composers began notating more specific levels of dynamics in their music; adjusting the volume levels of the brass and percussion to accommodate the characteristics of these instruments; marking the woodwind dynamic levels higher because of their difficulty projecting on solo passages; and scaling the string dynamic levels according to the size of the section and the overall orchestration of the music.

One of your responsibilities before you begin to rehearse a piece is to spend time evaluating, and perhaps adjusting, the dynamic markings in the music. You may need to change some of the volume levels for the musical voicings to emerge more clearly. Brass instruments naturally project louder than woodwinds, so the dynamics between those instruments may need adjusting. In any piece, all of the musical dynamics are relative. The volume of a *forte* depends on the size of your ensemble, the size of your performing space, and the scoring of the musical selection being considered. A "soloistic" passage should always be performed much louder than an accompaniment section.

Musicians must also be taught to listen and adapt their volume levels to others in the group. If a melody is passed from one musician to another, each must start the phrase at the same dynamic level as the previous instrument, or vocal section, so that the phrases match. Balancing dynamics is more about listening and adjusting, as if you are playing chamber music, than it is about playing strictly what is written on the page.

As a conductor, it is your responsibility to inspire your musicians to expand their concept of dynamic levels. Most ensembles play everything within a basic *mezzo-forte* level. They do not like to play extremely loud, and they hate to play softly. The best performances are defined by the contrast of the dynamic levels in the music. By insisting on a broader range of sound, you will increase the musicianship of your performers, and your music making will be more interesting and engaging.

Showing Dynamics

Understanding dynamics musically and communicating dynamics are two different things. To convey a certain dynamic level, you must develop excellent right- and left-hand independence and an understanding of how the size, weight, and placement of a beat can communicate various levels of volume to the musicians.

Dynamics

- Size
- Weight
- Low and High
- Close and Far

Video 5.6

Size

The technique for conducting dynamics can be approached by considering both the size and weight of the beat pattern. The easiest way to communicate dynamics is the concept that if you beat larger, the musicians will play louder, and if you beat smaller, the group will play softer. This approach can achieve good dynamic results. Experiment with conducting large patterns to communicate *forte* and smaller beat patterns to communicate *piano* dynamics.

Weight

Another way to view dynamics is in terms of the intensity, or weight, of the beat. A *forte* dynamic level can be shown quite effectively with either a larger or small beat pattern if the gesture is instilled with weight and intensity. A *pianissimo* dynamic can be conducted with either a small gesture or a large one if the gesture is light and flowing without weight. Altering the size and weight will also affect the speed of the gesture. Therefore, even though we associate speed with tempo, speed can also influence dynamics when related to the size and intensity of the beat.

See if you can communicate a change in dynamics through weight and speed as you practice conducting *pianissimo* with a large, light beat, and *fortissimo* with a small, heavy beat. Experiment with a variety of weight and resistance levels to see how this affects the perceived dynamics.

Placement of the Beat

Low and High

The placement of the beat pattern is another effective means of communicating dynamic levels and sudden changes of dynamics. We tend to associate a low beat with a *forte* sound and a higher beat with a *piano* sound; this works well, but it can also be reversed. When you are conducting a very soft phrase, you might conduct smaller beats with your hands low to create a feeling of intimacy. In contrast, it is also possible to conduct a *forte* passage with your hands held quite high. This is especially effective with the brass section while using a large beat so that it can be clearly seen. Experiment with communicating different volume levels with your hands held both low and high.

Close and Far

You can also move your hands closer or farther from your body to show a change in dynamics. In general, bringing your hands in closer will achieve a softer sound, while moving your hands farther from your body will create a more expansive volume as it increases your ability to utilize more sweep and weight.

As you practice showing dynamic levels using these concepts, remember that you should not move other parts of your body to signal changes in dynamics. Some conductors bend their knees trying to influence a softer dynamic level, or they stand on their tiptoes for a *fortissimo*; others might lean in toward the players in a sort of a crouching stance to signal softer playing or singing. All of these extraneous body motions interfere with the music making and send double signals to your performers. Eliminate these extraneous gestures from your technique and always communicate dynamics with your hands and arms alone.

Changing Dynamics

When you desire to show a gradual change of dynamics, you will combine many of the ideas and beat placement positions already mentioned. In addition, the left hand can be especially useful in encouraging musicians to play, or sing, *crescendos* and *diminuendos*. (See Video 5.7. ▶)

CRESCENDOS

Crescendos can be shown through a combination of gradually making the beat larger, adding more weight and resistance, and moving the gesture lower and outward from your body. Depending on the amount of crescendo desired, you might use all of these techniques, or you may incorporate only one or two of them.

You can also utilize the left hand to conduct a crescendo. Practice showing crescendos with your left hand while your right hand maintains a steady pulse. Use a metronome to help you pace the motions over a variety of measures or beat counts.

Exercises:

- Balance an object in the palm of your left hand and lift it up slowly. Practice this first by counting to 4 as you lift your hand. Then extend the length by counting to 6, then 8, 12, and 16, as you gradually lift your hand. Keep the motion smooth and connected.
- Practice the same exercise again, but experiment with imagining holding a variety of different weights in your hand. Hold and lift a marble, then a small rock, a larger rock, then imagine lifting an anvil. This sense of weight correlates to the volume and musical texture desired from the ensemble.

DIMINUENDOS

Diminuendos with the right hand can be conducted by gradually making the beat smaller, reducing the perception of weight and resistance, and by moving your hands closer to your body.

To conduct a diminuendo with your left hand, start with your hand high with the palm facing down, then gradually move your hand downward imagining that it is moving slowly through water. It is important to convey this resistance in the motion. Can you continue moving your left hand evenly without bouncing it up and down to the pulse? Strive for long, continuous, and even motions to show a diminuendo over the course of many bars.

If the music calls for a diminuendo down to silence at the end of a piece or a musical section, you can keep moving your hand lower and lower, until your hand is all the way down by your side. This continuation of the gesture can be very effective.

Exercises:

- Imagine a long light-dimmer switch, perhaps as long as a foot. With the palm of your left hand facing down, move the dimmer switch slowly downward. As you do this, count to 4, then try the same motion over 6, 8, 12, and 16 counts. Make sure that you always move your hand slowly and evenly.

- Practice the same gesture with additional weight and resistance. You should feel as if you are pressing down on the switch, but it is very tight and does not move easily. Connect to this feeling of resistance as you move your hand downward against it.

Phrasing

Every melody contains a central point that is the focus of the musical phrase. After that point is reached, the remaining notes of the melody and phrase are released. Conducting the phrasing of a melodic line is similar to conducting mini-crescendos and mini-diminuendos. Making these gestures natural and effective is difficult unless you have mastered your right- and left-hand independence. As your right hand shows the basic pulse, you can practice shaping the contour of a musical phrase with your left hand by applying the following gestures. (See Video 5.8. ▶)

Small Motions Sideways, with Weight—To gently add extra emphasis to specific notes in a phrase.

- Moving a coin on a table
- Pressing on a wet sponge and sliding it sideways

Motions Sideways, with Release—To help lift the musical line. This is applied to either a small group of notes or an entire phrase.

- Petting a mouse
- Petting a cat
- Brushing a horse

Arc Motions—To emphasize movement from one note to another; to shape the melodic line; or to bring out a specific harmonic change.

- Tracing a dome arc shape in the air
- Tracing the bottom of a bowl in the air (*palm downward*)
- Tracing the bottom of a bowl in the air (*palm upward*)

Finger Wiggles—To encourage lightness in a phrase, or to secure the attention of the musicians before continuing with the diminuendo.

- Wiggling your fingers as if you are drying them in the air

Free Motions—To encourage a lifted and free sound.

- Using random upward motions of the left hand

Sudden Dynamic Changes

Unexpected, or sudden, dynamic changes occur often in music. You must anticipate these types of changes by commanding the group's attention with your eyes while not disrupting your current volume level. It is important to show the difference in the dynamic level clearly with the preparatory beat that precedes the change. A late gesture, like a "thank-you" cue given after the player has begun to play the dynamic change is not effective for controlling the volume of the sound. Everything must be shown before the sound is produced.

Dynamic Changes

- Soft to Loud
- Loud to Soft
- Sforzandos

Video 5.9 ▶

Soft to Loud

When preparing for a *fortissimo* section or entrance that happens in the middle of a *piano* passage, your preparatory beat should be powerful, but small in size, and given directly in front of your body to hide it from the audience. You must never give away the surprise of a sudden *forte* entrance.

Example:

Preparatory beat	Show a small ictus, like shaking water off your fingers, followed by a larger rebound in order to place your hand in the correct position for the next gesture, which is the *forte* downbeat or side beat motion.
Downbeat/Side beat	After the rebound of a small ictus beat, show a sudden large gesture like slamming the trunk of the car closed for a vertical beat, or quickly wiping everything off a table for a horizontal beat.

Loud to Soft

If you are conducting a *forte* dynamic that suddenly changes to a *piano* or *pianissimo*, make sure that you do not anticipate the *piano* dynamic too early. It is best not to give a preparatory beat for this dynamic change. Instead, you can actually freeze, or stop your beat precisely when you want the change to occur. This sudden lack of motion will signal the change in the dynamic levels for the ensemble.

Exercise:

- Begin conducting with a large beat similar to bouncing a basket-ball, then suddenly stop on the beat itself using a hatchet motion that cancels out the rebound. After this momentary stop, lift and place your finger on the imaginary wall in front of you with a slight tap. To show a continued *piano* dynamic, repeat this tapping motion on the wall with a very small gesture.

To create a faster dynamic change, such as *fp*, you can show a strong accented gesture for the *forte*, then pull the rebound quickly back toward your body with a sudden stop. This will convey the release of the sound for the *piano*. After showing the *piano* dynamic, immediately return to the same size gestures you were conducting before the *fp* occurred.

Exercise:

- Bounce the basketball again, then suddenly stop your hand halfway through the rebound gesture while bringing your hand closer to your body. Conduct one smaller motion, and then return to bouncing the basketball.

Sforzandos

Sforzandos, like other dynamic markings, are always related to the overall dynamics of the music. They are not single-note *forte* markings, and they should never sound musically forced, or out of place. The important thing to remember with sforzandos is that they *must be played within the overall dynamic marking for the passage in which they occur.* So often, conductors assume that all sforzandos are played *forte*, or very loudly. A sforzando is basically a forced or accented note, or chord. A general rule for interpreting a sforzando marking is that *a sforzando should be played one dynamic marking above the level of the phrase in which it is placed.* Therefore, a sforzando in a *piano* passage should not be played more than *mezzo-forte*. All too often, the lyrical line of a phrase is ruined by performers playing an overzealous *sfz*.

You can emphasize a sforzando in a variety of ways. You can use a gesture that presses slightly down on the sound of the note, similar to a stressed accent, or you can actually lift the sound and emphasize the continued ring of the note. You also might perform a sforzando by adding a slightly different color to the sound, such as a wider or more prevalent vibrato. This is especially effective with sforzandos for the string players in soft lyrical passages. Last, you can change the *sfz* attack of the sound by encouraging your performers to incorporate a variety of bowing, or tonguing, techniques.

Examples of Sforzandos

Accented sforzando	Flicking water off your fingers or baton (*downward energy*)
Accented sforzando	Touching and reacting to a hot stove (*upward energy*)
Pressed sforzando	Pressing down on a wet sponge and releasing
Lifted sforzando	Dipping your fingers or baton in the cake batter and lifting them up

We have now covered an extensive list of gestures and explored how they can be applied to conducting. We have outlined some universal conducting rules, along with numerous exercises for fine-tuning your conducting technique. It is important to spend time practicing these exercises every day, training the muscles of your hands and arms, just like an athlete or a dancer. It is only through continuous repetition that you will be able to master a variety of gestures and use them naturally, without stress.

In the next section, we will explore relaxation and breathing concepts that conductors must be familiar with that can help focus the energy of their ensembles.

Becoming Centered

Have you ever wondered why some conductors are so compelling on stage? They have a confidence and a presence that radiates to the musicians and audience. Other conductors might come across as tense, mechanical, understated, or perhaps even boring. They do not have that special aura.

Your sense of presence on the concert stage has nothing to do with how much you move around on the podium, or even how well you know the score, although thorough knowledge of the musical score is essential for creating a high-quality performance. There is another element that constitutes this special ability to communicate the music passionately to others.

The people who are inspirational and dynamic in their conducting often do not know how they achieve this. They have come to it naturally. In sports, it is called being in the "zone." To enter this zone regularly, conductors must be totally relaxed and able to focus their minds solely on the music. They cannot be worried or stressed about the results. They have to know their craft so well that everything happens seemingly without effort.

This does not come naturally to everyone, but we can all learn a sense of peaceful presence. Achieving this state, however, may require a different approach to life. The first step is to focus on your breathing.

THE BREATH

Proper breathing is essential for conducting and also for remaining in a calm state of mind. Two areas are involved in breathing: your upper chest and your abdomen. When we become nervous, as we often are when we stand in front of a group, our shoulders tend to rise and our breathing becomes very shallow, keeping the air in our upper chest. Maintaining a deep sense of calm is facilitated by breathing deeply from the abdomen, not the upper chest. One must diligently practice proper breathing techniques so that breathing deeply becomes second nature. These exercises can be practiced anywhere, at any time. Therapeutic breathing skills will enhance your conducting and will also overflow into other aspects of your life.

Basic Breathing

When you practice breathing exercises, it is important that you empty all the air from your lungs before starting. Exhale fully and wait a little while before you begin to inhale. Breathe in slowly through the nose, keeping the shoulders down and allowing the air to extend the abdomen. Once your lungs are full, hold your breath for a while, the longer the better, then breathe out as slowly as possible through your mouth. When all the air is exhaled, wait a moment, then breathe in again through your nose and repeat these steps until you have established a relaxed rhythm. As you practice, try to extend the length of time that you breathe in and try to hold your breath longer before you exhale. Your goal is to slow your breathing down and to focus completely on breathing deeply from the abdomen.

Abdominal Breathing

As you refine your breathing technique, your physical body will actually change. Abdominal breathing can reduce your blood pressure, lower your heart rate, instill more oxygen, and slow your brain waves. Here are some steps to facilitate deep breathing from the abdomen.

- Wear loose-fitting clothes, or loosen your belt buckle around your waist.
- Relax all of your muscles as you take a deep breath, allowing the air to flow into the abdomen without moving your chest muscles.
- Place your hand below your navel so that you can feel the expansion of your abdomen each time you take a breath.
- Allow your stomach muscles to expand naturally.
- Once the abdomen is filled with air, allow the chest to fill with air and expand outward.

Benefits of breathing from your abdomen:

- Breathing slower will eliminate extraneous, stressful thoughts, allowing you to focus more effectively.
- By relaxing the muscles in your stomach, you will relax other muscles in your body.
- By utilizing this type of deep breathing, you will increase the oxygen in your blood, which will give you more energy. Consequently, you will feel more grounded as you conduct and more alive.

Side-to-Side Breathing

You can also practice breathing exercises that involve focusing the breath on one side of your body, and then moving the air to the other side.

As you are sitting or standing, use your finger to hold closed your left nostril, and at the same time, breathe in deeply through your right nostril. As you feel your right lung expand, focus your thoughts on to the right side of your body. Imagine that the air is filling up and extending out on that entire side. Now, close your right nostril and exhale all of your air from your left nostril. Experience the air releasing and contracting downward through the left side of your body. Make sure that you exhale all of your air. As you repeat this exercise, you should experience the feeling of a circle of air coming in and up one side of your body, then releasing down and out the other side.

Fast Breathing Exercise

Here is an exercise that will quickly put more oxygen into your system, as well as introduce you to another breathing technique.

Slowly breathe in and out normally while relaxing your body. When you are ready, breathe in through your nose and then quickly exhale through your nose with a short, sharp push. Quickly follow this with a very quick breath in. Repeat this fast breathing, in and out, through your nose about 25 times. It should take you only about 10 seconds. While you are doing this, you should feel as though your lungs are bellows of air that are being pushed and pulled.

Once you have finished this series of fast breaths through your nose, take a long, deep breath in to fill and expand your abdomen. As you slowly breathe out again, focus on any tingling or new sense of energy you can feel in your body. Repeat these slow, deep breaths six times. After you have finished, start the whole process over again, always breathing through your nose.

Counting Inhale and Exhale

To release more stress from your body, try this breathing exercise. The goal is to expel all your stress and tension with each breath.

Breathe in for four counts; hold your breath for seven counts. When finished, breathe out through your mouth for eight counts with your tongue against your upper teeth creating a "sss" sound. Wait after you have expelled all of your air for four counts, and then repeat this breathing exercise. Each time you exhale, imagine that you are pushing the negative energy out of your body.

Expanding Time between Your Breaths

This next exercise is good for tuning into, and increasing, your level of inner energy.

Breathe in deeply for six counts. Hold your breath for three counts, exhale for six counts. Before breathing in again, hold your breath for three counts, then repeat the process. As you continue the exercise, gradually increase the number of seconds that you are inhaling, and at the same time, expand the time between your breaths to be equal to half of the length that you are breathing in (8:4, 10:5, 12:6, 14:7, etc.). With practice, you will be able to slow your breathing tremendously. As you work through this exercise, you will experience your body becoming more relaxed, grounded, and centered.

Floor Breathing Exercise

Breathing on the floor is a good way to fully relax your body. After completing this exercise, you may feel as if the earth has literally pulled all of your tension away.

Lie down on the floor and feel yourself gradually settle against the ground. Try to release the muscle tension in your back and shoulders, so that your body is fully connected to the floor. Now, practice five minutes of deep breathing from your abdomen. (You may want to set a timer since time passes slowly when you do this exercise.) Breathe in through your nose as you count to eight. Hold your breath for four counts, then exhale for 10 counts or longer. Wait as long as possible and empty out all of your air completely before drawing your next breath and repeating the exercise. Your body should become steadily more relaxed. After the five minutes, remain on the floor for a few more minutes as you resume normal breathing. Feel how your body has released tension, your thoughts have calmed, and your heart rate has slowed.

Standing Breathing Exercises

As a conductor, you will spend many hours standing, so it is important that you practice breathing exercises while upright. These techniques can later be applied during rehearsals and concerts.

GATHER AIR IN

As you are standing in a straight, but relaxed, manner, place your arms out to each side, and then gradually move them toward your chest as you breathe in deeply through your nose. Try to experience gathering the air around you. At the end of your inhale, rest your hands on your chest. Wait a few seconds, then exhale through your mouth with your hands remaining on your chest. Breathe in again with your hands still on your chest, and then, as you release the air, expand your arms out in front of you and move your arms to each side in a half circle as if you are doing the breaststroke. After releasing all your air, wait a few seconds in this position, then start over and breathe in as you move your arms again to rest on your chest. Repeat each step of the exercise. To end, move your arms and hands back to rest gently against your sides and tune in to any sensations you might be feeling.

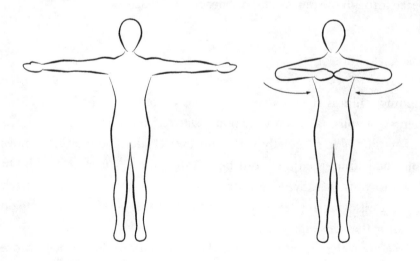

FINDING STILLNESS

As you develop a deeper sense of calm, you may discover that everything in the universe seems to be connected. The individual focus on *you* and *me* becomes less clear, and it is possible that you will become much more compassionate and accepting. Adopting this philosophy about life can transform the way you interact with your musical group and can make you a better musical leader.

Some people find their sense of stillness in nature; others find it through meditation, religion, or involvement with a church. Still others find it in solitude. Each of us knows deep inside what makes us feel peaceful and fulfilled, but so often the busyness of everyday life obstructs our development of a calm center.

As you strive to strengthen your inner stillness, you need to tune in to your qualities of love, inspiration, and creativity, and allow these wonderful attributes to flow from you to the members of your ensemble. These qualities become the inspiration for the music making. In finding stillness, you should be able to connect to your core being and your heart. From this perspective, you can speak and act honestly, and your fear of failure disappears. This will enable you to experience more quiet, joy, and peace through the music and to share this with others.

Releasing Tension

Finding stillness requires you to release all tension, whether physical, mental, or spiritual, from your body. One technique for releasing stress and tension is to sit quietly with your eyes closed, and gradually move your focus from the tip of your head, through every part of your body, down to your toes. Systematically identify each point and ask yourself if you are storing any tension there. If the answer is yes, concentrate on releasing that tension.

Start with the top of your head. What sensations do you feel? Move your attention to your eyes and your forehead. Spend a moment using the previous breathing exercises to release the tension stored there. Now concentrate on releasing your jaw, neck, and shoulders, and evaluate your arms, hands, and fingers, releasing any stress or tension that you feel. Then focus on your heart, lungs, abdomen, stomach, hips. Finish up with your legs, knees, ankles, and feet. Gradually work your way through every possible place where you could be harboring stress, and try to let it go.

IMAGINARY SHOWER

Your last step in fully releasing tension and re-energizing your body can be done by imagining that you are being washed and cleansed by an imaginary shower, similar to the tai chi exercise introduced in Chapter 1.

While standing, exhale, and imagine that all the tensions and problems you are carrying are being released downward. Feel this release of stress travel down through your body, out your feet, and into the ground.

Now, imagine the water of a shower pouring over your head. It is cascading off your hair and streaming down your shoulders. It washes everything negative down through your body and out into the earth below. As the shower is pouring over you, empty your lungs completely of all air. Wait a few seconds, let the shower stop, then breathe in again, and start the process over. As the imaginary water flows over your body, feel it cleansing your spirit. Let it melt away all your frustrations. Each time you feel the water wash over you, you will release even more tension and stress.

Quieting Your Mind

It is hard to develop an overall feeling of calm when you have so many details and distractions in your life. We all face this situation. It takes practice to learn how to quiet your mind. Do not expect to sit down and immediately feel *calm*. Instead, commit to spending 10 minutes per day in a quiet state.

For maximum effect, find a place to sit with no other distractions. You want to be comfortable, so you need a room that is not too cold, nor too hot. The chair should fit your body well and support your back.

Sometimes you might want to use a small pillow to place behind the lower part of your back for greater comfort.

Practice the following exercise to settle your mind. At first, you might feel nervous and impatient, and many thoughts might enter your mind all at once. Let these thoughts come and go, but do not focus on any of them as you sit and breathe deeply in and out. In the beginning, it will take a long time for you to achieve a calm state, but with practice, you will be able to settle your mind much more quickly. Following this outline is helpful when you are starting out.

- Sit quietly with your back straight in a comfortable position.
- Close your eyes and try to release any muscle tension you feel in your body.
- Breathe deeply in and out.
- Allow your thoughts to come and go, but do not dwell on them or make judgments.
- Repeat a positive word like "calm" or "peace" over and over to help focus your mind.
- Think of a place of beauty and imagine yourself in that place.
- For your first few times, set a timer for 10 minutes. Later on, try to expand this quiet time to 15 or 20 minutes.

QUIET STANDING

Some people practice a quiet standing exercise. This involves all the steps listed previously, but instead of sitting, you stand in one place with your feet grounded, with your head, neck, and back relaxed. This exercise is particularly good for conductors, since we need to develop the ability to stand in place without stress or tension for long periods of time.

As you practice standing, keep your weight equally balanced on both feet. Over time, there will be a tendency for you to want to shift from one foot to the other. You may also find that, as you stand, it is difficult to relax your shoulders. If you are experiencing this problem, go back and repeat some of the shoulder exercises listed earlier, until the tension is released.

For your standing exercise, first start with just five minutes, then work your way up to longer lengths. Eventually, you should be able to stand calmly for the duration of a Mahler symphony!

After you have achieved a calm stillness in your standing position, apply this stillness to your conducting. Begin to conduct some basic beat patterns while remaining calm and centered. Hear the music in your head as your arms show the gestures.

Now, imagine you are standing before a roomful of performers. In the beginning, this sensation of simply standing in front of a group can feel quite awkward. Your challenge is to remain calm and to focus the energy in the room. You need to become comfortable standing on the podium. Envision a packed audience in the concert hall behind you. Experiment with sending energy back and forth between your ensemble and your audience.

Freeing the Mind

While you are in this relaxed, quiet state, practice releasing your mind from busy and stressful thoughts. You must withdraw from thoughts of imminent success or concern about what others think. *Focus only on the music and the task at hand.* As you are getting ready to conduct, your entire body should be ready to sing with the music. Let the music flow through you to everyone around you.

LIVE IN THE MOMENT

To conduct a truly inspirational performance, you have to be fully present in the moment. So often, this ability is blocked by fears and insecurities. It is hard to stand in front of a group of musicians knowing that they are going to be critical of every motion you make, and every word you say. As you strive to become a conductor, many people will tell you that you do not have the talent, the background, the knowledge, the contacts, or the natural skill level necessary to achieve success. If you listen to these naysayers, you will practically drown from negative feedback.

You must always remember that other people's opinions are not reality. *You* create your own reality with your thoughts, and you create your own concept of success. If your intentions are honest and you are connected to your inner soul, you can always enjoy sharing your gift of music making with others.

To be freely "in the moment" you also need to know the music so well that you are released from the physical score. You cannot be bogged down with thoughts of whom to cue when, and with worry about whether the musicians will play or sing in tune. You have to trust that they will perform all the right notes at the right time and encourage them to do their job. The establishment of trust between conductor and musicians is what allows all of you to contribute your best performance.

Recognize Your Fears

It is important that you recognize your fears directly instead of trying to cover them up with a false confidence that often comes across as arrogant or demeaning on the podium. Fear creates stress and tension in the body, which can negatively impact your ability to communicate. It is best if you can accept your fears and focus mentally on releasing the thoughts that are holding you back. These might be concerns about your abilities, or feelings that the world will never give you a break. Instead of constantly trying to manipulate events, simply strive to fully enjoy the current moment.

Accept Your Situation

Our minds are constantly analyzing and trying to solve problems in order to move us forward toward our goals. As we grow up, we are taught that we must work hard and think hard. We are taught that to achieve and to succeed we must control our lives and think our way to success. Our minds are perpetually busy. This approach to life can be very stressful when things are not going our way.

The reality is that we cannot control many situations in life. If you believe that your happiness is related strictly to achieving all of your goals, you may live a very stressful life. When you accept situations and appreciate them for what they are, much of your stress will immediately be released. This acceptance is essential for building a connection to your inner energy. It is the first step for getting into that *zone* we were discussing earlier.

This acceptance will release you from emotional involvements that can cloud your decision-making process. Sometimes we simply have to remove ourselves emotionally from the outcomes of a situation. I call this *"getting out of our own way."* If you can accept where you are now, you will become more open and flexible to new possibilities.

Quiet Your Inner Critic

To say that you are going to accept things as they are, and to actually accomplish it, are two very different things. Each of us has an "inner voice" that gives us a steady, running commentary about how we perceive what we are doing in the world. Because our training as musicians has been so intense, we are usually very self-critical. It is essential to develop a sense of emotional detachment and the ability to calm your constant stream of negative thoughts.

Redefine Your Reality

This requires that you redefine the thoughts that *you* allow into your mind. You cannot always change your current situation, but you can change your reaction to it. Stress and negative beliefs affect the whole person. To shift your views from the negative to the positive is difficult to do, but this simple shift can change your life dramatically. Strive to view everything from the most positive perspective possible.

Many athletes have perfected the ability to concentrate on positive images before each game and to view their actions on the field with a focused detachment. Musicians must do the same. As a conductor and artistic leader, you must generate a positive enthusiasm for life in all situations, and do not allow yourself to be dragged into controversy and emotional issues. See how this shift in attitude and perspective alters the environment for your rehearsals.

Center Your Attention

Successful conductors have an excellent ability to focus. The problem is that we are usually focusing on the wrong things. Instead of worrying about the infinite number of details involved with making music, experiment with conveying that outward sense of calm.

CANDLE FLAME

A good method for beginning to understand calm focus is to stare for a long time at the flame of a lighted candle. The longer you stare, the more the outside world disappears and you begin to sense a feeling of tranquility inspired by the simplicity of the flame. You are living in that moment only, not dwelling on the past or present. Practice this simple exercise daily until you can achieve this same type of focused state without the candle and apply this to your conducting.

The challenge, of course, is to be able to exude a calm focus, yet at the same time convey the details needed to perform your job as a conductor. Luckily, most conductors have the ability to divide their attention easily. It is almost as if you are watching yourself work from a separate vantage point from your body.

Tune in to Your Body

It is a challenge to tune into your body and to train yourself to perceive gentle shifts in energy, tension, and release. You rely on your body to communicate your musical ideas to the musicians, so you need the skills to be aware of its every aspect.

See if you can sense other vibrations or sensations in your body: a feeling of warmth or coolness, a tingling sensation, or perhaps enlivened energy. Are you aware of colors, sounds, tastes, or smells? Work your way through all of your senses as you build a stronger awareness of your body. To help yourself focus on these areas, you might try asking yourself questions. *What am I feeling now? Do I sense tension in my shoulder? What color keeps coming up in my mind? Is there a tingling sensation in my fingers?* Gradually examine the different parts of your body and see how the sensations you experience might influence your conducting.

TUNING INTO UNIVERSAL ENERGY

Your goal on the podium is to radiate a sense of confidence and a relaxed alertness. Imagine that your body is like a garden hose. When the hose is straight, the water flows through freely, but when it is kinked and twisted, the water flow will be reduced or even stopped entirely. This is analogous to the way that we communicate energy to our ensemble. When we are too tense and our body is "kinked," the music becomes trapped within us instead of flowing out smoothly to the musicians. This blockage of the energy can cause stress and lifelong muscle problems.

To conduct beyond the surface of the music, you must be able to convey your inner energy, not only to the musicians in front of you but also to the audience behind you. The core of this energy comes from deep in your psyche. You must learn how to enliven this energy and send it out, like water through a garden hose, into the room around you.

Grounding Yourself

As we conduct, we want to feel grounded and connected to the earth through the conductor's podium. A way to increase this connection is to release all of our negative energy downward through exercises like the

Imaginary Shower. After you have released this negative energy, imagine that you are pulling energy upward out of the earth that is solid and clean. Imagine that you are a plant, or a tree, that is growing and drawing its nutrients from the soil. Feel this nourishment and energy flow up through your body and be refreshed.

Establishing Your Energy Field

Each of us is surrounded by a field of energy that radiates to the people with whom we come in contact. Sometimes this concept is difficult for people to understand. Remember the energy example of rubbing your hands together as if you are going to warm them from Chapter 3? After you rub them together, separate the hands and move them to both sides of your body, about chest high with the palms facing each other, and start to move them slowly toward each other. Stop when you start to feel a resistance in the air. Some people will feel this resistance when the hands are two to three feet apart; others may not feel resistance until their hands are one foot apart; and for a few, the hands might be as close as six inches apart before resistance is sensed. This exercise gives you a basic sense of the size and power of your energy field.

Work on expanding your energy field so that it will flow more freely to the musicians and the audience. As you are standing, imagine that your entire body is a beacon of light. This light stretches from you in all directions and fills the entire room. Experiment with controlling this beacon of light. Can you make it larger and brighter? Can you reduce it? Focus on how you are making these changes. What are you thinking? How does your body feel as you are creating these different sensations?

A fully relaxed, energized yet focused body is essential for all conductors. Strive to master your breathing and your posture, and be able to control and communicate your sense of personal energy to the people around you. A calm, centered body is essential for effective conducting.

7

Making Music

COMMUNICATING THE MUSIC

A good conductor has a strong musical concept to communicate to the ensemble. This concept involves defining the emotions and character that the music portrays. To convey emotion, you must *feel* it personally. Identifying with your inner feelings is difficult because it exposes part of your soul. Not only must you feel these emotions yourself, but you must convincingly communicate these emotions to the musicians in front of you, not through words, but through your gestures.

Conveying Emotions

To convey emotions, you will need to draw from your own experiences of love, anger, sorrow, and joy, to name just a few. You must know the quality of the sound you want to evoke in order to portray a specific feeling, and you must develop the conducting technique required to inspire that specific sound. With each of the following emotions, experiment with feeling this emotion and assign it a sound quality in your head. Then identify gestures and facial expressions that you feel clearly communicate each emotion.

Joy
Think about a time when you were incredibly happy. Feel what changes in your body as you remember this time or situation. Focus on this visual image and physical feeling. Now think of a piece of music that fits with

that mood. Practice dancing and moving as you express your feelings of joy to this piece of music. Do not be afraid to physically exude this emotion in order to understand how to communicate it to others. Draw on these feelings and memories the next time you conduct music that is joyful.

EXCITEMENT

Was there ever something that you just couldn't wait to do? When you couldn't sleep at night because you were so excited about what was going to happen the next day? Recreate that feeling now in your body. Relive that day visually in your memory. Now think of music that fits with that feeling. Try to identify two or three different pieces. Hear this music in your head while experiencing this excitement. Feel the thrill flowing through your body and out the end of the baton as you conduct. If you were a person observing your own gestures right now, would you feel excitement? Memorize this feeling so you can utilize it later on.

SADNESS

There are moments in life for all of us that are tragic. Focus on a memory of something that hurt you deeply; the death of a loved one, the loss of a job, a major failure of some type. Feel the weight of this emotion. Breathe deeply and let the heaviness pull the muscles of your body downward. Think now of a piece of music that conveys this type of emotion. Conduct a few phrases from that piece. Can you feel the density of sadness? Can you hear the texture of the sound?

LONELINESS

This emotion is similar to sadness, but without the weight. It is a more hollow, empty feeling. Recreate a memory of a time when you were lonely. Feel the emptiness and space. How is this feeling different from sadness? How is it different from joy? As you look for music that expresses loneliness, try to analyze the reason you think a specific piece, or movement, is related to this emotion. Conduct a portion of this piece and feel the calm of loneliness flowing through your body. See if you can communicate this feeling to the group in front of you.

OTHER FEELINGS

Make a list and experiment with other emotions and feelings, or states that elicit them. Some to start with are love, tragedy, humor, awe, beauty, and anger. Can you find ways to physically feel and experience these emotions in your body? Practice communicating these feelings through the weight and resistance in your gestures. As you do this, be careful not to distort your face or body. Your face can be used to express the overall emotion, but this expression should be subtle and natural. It should stem from the true emotion coming through you, and not as if from a mask put on by a bad actor in a play.

Communicating Character

How does the character of a piece differ from the emotions it might evoke? When I think of character, I think of words like bold, dashing, playful, and noble. These are words that describe an action rather than a feeling. How does one convey musical character with gestures alone?

Mimes convey character by actually changing their body posture. They can shift from portraying an old man to a young child just by the way they hold their bodies and by their movements. As a conductor, you must do something similar, except that the space in which you make your gestures is much more limited.

To show character, you must never change your basic posture; instead, through varying the size, energy, weight, speed, and resistance of your conducting motion, you can show different types of characters, thus enhancing the interpretation of the music. Here are a few examples to experiment with:

Fiery	A large, fast motion, without too much weight or resistance
Imposing	A slow, heavy, ponderous motion
Bold	A confident, large motion with lots of energy
Calm	A smooth motion that is light in feel, but very connected

Experiment with conveying different character traits in musical pieces and come up with some character examples on your own to practice. See if someone watching you can guess what type of musical character you are communicating with your gestures.

Guiding with a Light Touch

Regardless of the feeling of weight and resistance that is necessary to portray character and emotion in music, you also want to be able to guide your ensemble with a light and very sensitive touch.

RIDING A THOROUGHBRED

I often compare conducting a group of musicians to riding a Thoroughbred horse. Even if you do not ride, I think you will understand the analogy. To ride a Thoroughbred, you have to use a light tough on the reins. The smallest movement of your hand communicates volumes to an experienced racehorse. Your body should be balanced and relaxed, allowing you to be totally connected to the horse you are riding and not obstructing him. You need to be gentle and encouraging, but also firm. You must respect that the horse is well trained and eager to perform well. As you ride, you are constantly aware of the shifting muscles of the animal and you must focus on connecting to that energy. You must know how to guide the horse in the right direction, when to give it a nudge forward, when to let the reins out, and when to hold it back.

When you are riding a Thoroughbred horse, you are always aware that it is the horse that is running the race; *you* are not running the race. The jockey should never get in the way of what the horse needs to do; extraneous motions just confuse and slow it down. The wrong gestures, balance, or position will cause you to lose the race, no matter how fast the horse. You must encourage and allow the horse to run its best at all times, just as you must allow and inspire the members of your ensemble to perform their best.

RIDING A MULE

Many of us, however, conduct as if we were riding a mule. We do not trust the animal to go forward in the right direction. We kick and yank on the reins, right and left. We scream and shout at it and send confusing and contradictory signals. We blame it for not going fast enough; for going in the wrong direction; or for not reading our minds. We tell it to go forward, but send signals at the same time that pull back on the reins and instruct it to slow down. We are not balanced and poised, but instead clumsy and awkward, making it more difficult for the mule to run. Riding a mule is all about us and what we want. There is no feeling of trust or respect. Conductors of this type will always blame their ensemble for not being good enough, even though the fault is usually their own.

CONDUCTING CONSIDERATIONS

As a conductor, it is important that you master a variety of gestures and develop a solid conducting technique; however, you must also study the music appropriately so that you *know exactly what you are trying to communicate* to your musicians.

You will do most of this prior to actually conducting an ensemble. Every conductor must spend numerous hours carefully studying and analyzing each musical score. You must decide on an interpretation that encompasses the melodic and harmonic relationships as well as the overall form of the piece. This includes making decisions regarding where the most important musical ideas are and how you plan to bring these out. You must have a defined sense of the tone color and phrasing you would like to achieve, and you must ingrain in your mind an inner sense of rhythm so that you can conduct the same basic tempos each time you rehearse or perform a section. Also, you must make sure that your tempos are *right* for the music so that you do justice to the composer's musical vision.

Score Study

There are many philosophies on studying and marking your scores. Some people use a system of color pencils; others use very specific visual markings that they can see at a glance. What is most important is not how you mark your score, but that you know the music.

Many schools of thought advocate that you work your way through the score a number of times, each time focusing on a different aspect of the piece in order to develop a deeper understanding of the music. Every time you study a score, you will discover more nuances and inner relationships. It is best if you can memorize most of your scores to enable you to have more eye contact with the musicians. Here are some ideas to help you with your score study.

Overview of the Score

- Examine the instrumentation and know the transpositions of the instruments utilized.
- Read all of the composer's notes and setup diagrams, plus any editor comments or notations.
- Decide on the basic tempos and establish tempo relationships between sections and movements. Write these down in the score.
- Translate and understand all terms, musical instructions, and special notations.

First Read-Through

- Go through the entire piece either on a piano or another instrument, or hear it in your head.
- Acquire a general impression of the form and harmonic structure of the piece.
- Identify the essential mood or emotions of the music that you will communicate.

Analyze the Music

- Make a detailed chart of the overall form and the musical structure of the piece.
- Write down a harmonic analysis and an evaluation of the harmonic relationships of the larger sections.
- Identify the main melodies, themes, and motives, along with their instrumentation. Evaluate why these specific instruments were chosen.

- Analyze the musical direction and high points of individual phrases, and mark the breathing points.
- Identify the rhythmic challenges, both for you and for the performers. Physically practice difficult meter changes and transitions.
- Understand the dynamics throughout the piece. Analyze the balance between the different instruments in specific sections, the musical climaxes, unusual articulations, and special effects.
- Study the overall orchestration, texture, tessitura, and tone colors. Decide which tonal colors are most important to bring out, and why.

DECIDE ON AN INTERPRETATION

- Research performance practice for that composer and style period.
- Research the history of the piece and what was happening in the composer's life at that time.
- Make final decisions on tempos and musical climax points incorporating what you have learned.
- Place bowings into the string parts, or work with your principal players to establishing the bowings for each section.
- Finalize the specific seating arrangement, or stage setup, that works best for this piece.
- Define and practice the gestures that will be most effective to communicate the mood, character, emotion, and energy of different sections of this composition.
- Study the music until you are able to hear the entire piece in your head.

For vocal pieces, because of the addition of text and the limitations of the human voice, there are a few more categories that you must cover as you work on analyzing and preparing the music.

- Assess the vocal ranges and musical contour (scales and awkward intervals) of the piece.
- Translate, or locate a quality translation of, the text if the piece utilizes a foreign language.

- Mark the breaths and specific cutoffs for all phrases.
- Make decisions on diction and the pronunciation of vowels and consonants. Mark these into your score and provide a marked score or part for your singers.

Rehearsal and Concert Preparation

As you select music and prepare for rehearsals and concerts, you will need to make decisions on specific details so that the rehearsal and concert experience will be successful for everyone involved. Here is a breakdown of items to consider and incorporate.

CHOICE OF REPERTOIRE

Room/Hall	Evaluate the size of the stage, the concert hall, and the acoustics. Make sure that you select music that will work well in that space.
Audience	What type of concert are you performing and what are the expectations of the audience? Consider the length, musical complexity, and the accessibility of the proposed repertoire, as well as the age of the audience and their educational background.
Strengths	What is the quality and experience level of the ensemble? Carefully evaluate their strengths and weaknesses. How can you showcase their strengths?
Schedule	How much rehearsal time will you have? Can the pieces you have selected be rehearsed in this amount of time? Over what time period do these rehearsals take place?
Budget	How many musicians, rehearsals, and performances can you afford? How many concerts are you allowed to do? Do you have a budget for rental music? Will you need to rent any additional instruments or equipment to perform these pieces? What extra performers might be needed?

Before the Rehearsals Begin

Music
You should always specify which edition you would like to use and make sure that your bowings, vocal pronunciations, or specific markings are transferred into the musicians' parts. Make sure to check the placement of rehearsal letters or measure numbers in the parts against those in your score to confirm that they match.

Plan
Prepare a detailed schedule for every rehearsal. This schedule should be distributed to the musicians in advance. Follow the schedule and avoid making last-minute changes whenever possible.

Setup
It is best to provide a detailed setup diagram that the stage crew or setup person can follow. This will save you time and frustration later on.

Instructions
Make a list of any specific instructions that the musicians or stage crew might need to know for the pieces to be rehearsed or performed.

At the First Rehearsal

Dress
If this is your first time to appear in front of the ensemble, you will want to make a good impression. What is the appropriate dress for this group? You do not want to be overdressed, but you also do not want to be too casual. Anticipate what you think will fit in best with the type of group that you are conducting.

Issues
Last-minute issues with players missing or parts missing will always arise. Anticipate these problems and be ready to be flexible. Never lose your "cool" in front of your ensemble.

Comments
You can start the rehearsal with a few opening comments for the musicians. Keep your comments short and positive. Players are there to make music, not to hear you talk.

Rehearsal
Evaluate ahead of time what you want to accomplish during each rehearsal. Will you run through all the pieces, or start rehearsing on the hardest piece right away? Plan your time carefully in advance so that you will use it wisely. Do not spend all your time on one piece at the sacrifice of another piece on the program. Musicians appreciate being well prepared on all the pieces.

Breaks
Be sure that you know what time you are required to take a break. It is important to be familiar with the normal schedule of the group and to take the breaks at the proper times to avoid musicians becoming tired or frustrated.

REHEARSAL TECHNIQUES

Comments   As you rehearse, use positive and constructive comments. It is also important that you speak slowly so that the musicians have time to absorb your words and that the rehearsal does not feel frantic.

Pauses   Be sure to pause before you give instructions to the orchestra. They need time to focus, and the sound in the room needs time to settle so that everyone can hear what you are saying.

Pacing   Try to avoid having sections of players sitting for a long time without playing or singing. They will become bored or disengaged, and this will negatively impact the overall quality of the rehearsal.

Focus   Decide in advance whether you are going to focus on broad musical issues or specific details for each piece. Much of this will depend upon the amount of time available.

Repetition   If you have rehearsed a spot three times and it is not getting better, leave it and go on. There is a point at which things get worse, not better. You can always return to that spot later during the next rehearsal.

Tuning   When tuning chords, start with the musicians who play or sing the root of the chord, add the fifth of the chord, and then add the third of the chord last. Tuning sections in this manner allows the performers to understand how their note functions in the chord, and informs them regarding who else is playing their same note.

AFTER THE REHEARSAL

Evaluate   Spend time assessing what went well and which sections still need work. Make a specific list of items to cover in the next rehearsal and how much time each will need. Bookmark these spots carefully in your score so that you can find them quickly.

Plan   Incorporate your list of concerns from the preceding rehearsal and prepare a detailed plan of how you will spend your time on each piece for the next rehearsal. Be specific in allocating your time and assign how long you will rehearse each section, movement, or piece.

Changes   During a series of rehearsals for a concert, sometimes you will need more time on a piece than you originally anticipated. When making a schedule change, announce it clearly in advance, and if possible, e-mail the schedule change to everyone in the group so that they will be ready for the change.

Dress Rehearsal

Order

During the dress rehearsal, will you rehearse in concert order? Or from the largest instrumentation to the smallest, or smallest to largest? Consider both the musicians and the stage crew as you make your decisions about the order of the dress rehearsal. If the concert involves a lot of complex stage changes, it might be best to rehearse in concert order so that the crew can practice moving the equipment and the performers can better understand the flow of the concert.

Pacing

For the dress rehearsal, will you play everything straight through, or do you have time to rehearse? Sometimes you may only have time to start and end each piece. Make sure you are always sensitive to the endurance and physical limitations of your players, especially if the dress rehearsal is the same day as the concert.

Timing

Be aware of the timing of each piece, movement, and individual section that you might rehearse. You do not want to run out of time on a dress rehearsal. There is nothing worse than failing to finish a piece at the last rehearsal.

Audience

Some dress rehearsals are open to the public. If this is your situation, you might spend your time playing the pieces straight through instead of stopping and rehearsing. Know in advance if there will be an audience at the dress rehearsal so that you can plan appropriately.

Concert

Before

Make sure you reserve extra time before the concert for any last-minute emergencies that might occur. Always arrive at the hall early.

Allow yourself some quiet time to focus solely on the music before the concert. It is very important for you to have time to calm your mind and to find stillness.

You may be asked to be involved with pre-concert talks or receptions. Be sure to plan your time accordingly and keep an eye on the clock. It is easy to lose track of time at these events, and this may delay the start of the concert or compromise your quiet time before the performance.

During   Decide in advance if you will be talking during the concert and
                  inform the stage crew so they can set up a microphone. Prepare
                  in advance exactly what you will say to introduce yourself and
                  the music, and always perform a microphone check before the
                  concert begins.

                  Stay focused on the music, no matter what happens during
                  the performance. Unexpected mistakes will undoubtedly
                  occur; entrances may be missed or notes fumbled. Do not allow
                  these mishaps to distract you from the music itself and your
                  goal of inspiring the musicians to play at their highest level.

                  If you are guest-conducting an ensemble and the occasion
                  seems appropriate, publicly thank the ensemble before the last
                  piece on the program.

After   After the concert, stand backstage and shake hands with the
                  performers as they exit the stage. This goes a long way toward
                  building a good rapport with your ensemble.

                  If an after-concert reception is scheduled, be sure to at-
                  tend, and try not to keep people waiting too long. If you are
                  guest-conducting, ask that someone be available to introduce
                  you to important people, faculty members, large donors, staff
                  and board members.

Do's and Don'ts

Ever since we were young, we have been surrounded by rules and lists
of things that we should "*do*" and things we should "*not do*" in life. As
conductors, we are exposed to these same types of lists and expectations.
Following these basic *do's* and *don'ts* will help you to succeed as a conductor and will improve your ability to relate to your group of musicians.

Do

Physical
   Whenever possible, stand to conduct.
   Always conduct the first entrance very clearly.
   Always show clear downbeats. The musicians need to know where
      beat one is.
   Maintain good eye contact and allow your eyes to embrace everyone.

Always conduct to the back stands or rows of the group.

Communicate to your musicians with clear gestures and avoid irritating mannerisms.

Invite the musicians to play—do not demand.

Display an energetic, engaged demeanor during rehearsals and concerts.

Verbal

Keep stopping and talking to a minimum.

Know what you are stopping for and tell players clearly what you want them to do differently.

Speak only when the group is silent.

Be very specific with your comments.

Say "we" instead of "I" whenever possible.

Speak clearly and make sure that musicians in the back can hear you speak.

Look at the musicians, not at the score, when you are talking.

Give the musicians time to find the spot you are referring to.

Strive to keep your comments positive during the rehearsals.

Musical

Mark parts in advance of the first rehearsal.

Be sure your score and the group's scores contain the same letters or measure numbers.

Know the transpositions for the different instruments.

Know the English translations of all the musical instructions.

Demand a high standard from your ensemble.

Fine-tune small details at the beginning of a rehearsal to set a standard for the entire rehearsal.

Work first on notes and rhythm, then on dynamics and balance.

Always cue players or sections that have long rests.

Rehearse specific details up to three times, and then move on.

Atmosphere

Create a positive working environment.

Be respectful of your performers.

Use positive humor when appropriate.

Praise musicians for jobs well done.

Get to know the members of your ensemble.

Other Points to Remember

Breath is the motion of the music. Remember to breathe while you conduct.

Always tell the ensemble specifically what you want; do not criticize what they did.

The more difficult the rhythms in a piece, the clearer and simpler your gestures must be.

The less interesting the part, the more energy you and the performers need to use to perform it.

To Improve Yourself

Conduct as much as possible.

Join music organizations and attend conferences and workshops to broaden your knowledge.

Observe other conductors in rehearsals.

Study with different conductors and participate in master classes.

Travel as much as possible to expand your view of the world.

Attend concerts regularly.

Listen to many styles of music and study music from different style periods by a variety of composers.

Read books on music.

Know the history of the piece you are conducting.

Play or sing in a large ensemble regularly.

Take lessons on your own instrument.

Learn a secondary instrument, or take vocal lessons.

Don't

Physical

Don't over-conduct.

Don't make faces.

Don't mouth words, sing, or hum along.

Don't move your head or chin up and down with the music.

Don't move your feet.

Don't bend your knees.

Don't jump up and down.

Don't lick your fingers before you turn the pages of the score.

Don't brush your hair off your forehead.

Don't let your hair get in your eyes or cover your face.

Verbal

Don't talk too much or tell long stories on the podium.

Don't talk over noise; wait for silence.

Don't whisper.

Don't throw a fit, lose your temper, or show anger or frustration.

Don't belittle the musicians.

Don't say "you are out of tune."

Don't "ssh" the ensemble.

Don't tell them to watch you. Instead project what you want and they will be compelled to watch.

Musical

Don't be a metronome or a time-beater.

Don't accept mediocrity when your musicians are capable of more.

Don't repeat sections over and over without telling the musicians what you want done differently.

Don't stop for obvious wrong notes.

Don't learn the score in front of the ensemble.

Don't just conduct the melody.

Don't allow the ensemble to play or sing everything the same way; encourage musicality.

Don't conduct music you don't believe in.

Atmosphere

Don't waste players' time by stopping too often.

Don't let individual sections sit for too long without playing while you are rehearsing others.

Don't stop the ensemble if you created the problem because you made a mistake or were unclear.

INSPIRED LEADERSHIP

To inspire the people with whom you work and to guide them with a light touch, you need to establish a feeling of mutual trust. Most conductors lead through their position of power, expecting that everyone will do what they say because they are the boss. Unfortunately, this type of leadership does not inspire the best performances. It is better to develop a leadership style based on mutual respect. The musicians must trust you, and you must trust them. When they know that you believe in them, you will be able to inspire the group to play at its fullest potential.

Building Trust

Musicians can sense from the moment you step on the podium whether you respect them. Often, from insecurity or fear, a conductor will present an image of arrogance, or overconfidence, immediately alienating the members of the ensemble. You need to gain control of your emotions and fears before you conduct a musical group. If you are honest with the musicians, they will usually be honest with you. During rehearsals, do not be afraid to admit when you make a mistake. They probably already know it, and in admitting it openly, you will increase the musicians' respect for you. Treat the members of your ensemble with the same warmth and respect that you would accord a good friend or a close family member.

Invite Your Musicians to Play

When you conduct, do not demand, but rather invite the musicians to play. More important, allow them to play by avoiding mixed signals or confusing gestures. So often we force the sound or beat it to death and the players are required, like a group of marching soldiers, to simply put their notes in the right place—left, right, left, right, 1, 2, 3, 4. A great conductor shows emotion, character, tone quality, and precise tempo within his or her first preparatory beat, and in this way is able to inspire the group to make music from the very first note. These conductors lead quietly, becoming more active when needed and allowing the group to play freely with a very light touch when appropriate.

Less Is More

In this same line of thought, try not to be so "busy" as you are conducting. Conducting is not about beating time through every single measure. Some conductors are so involved with showing every cue, marking every dynamic contrast, and emphasizing every pulse in such a rigid fashion that one almost feels that they are conducting to the numbers, like a "paint-by-the-numbers" craft kit. If you are over beating, or wildly dancing to the music, the musicians will stop watching you, and they will be forced to make their own artistic decisions, which will create a very disjointed interpretation.

It is not necessary to emphasize every beat in a piece of music. Rather, it is important to know when to get out of the way. Believe it or not, the group will usually play just as well, and maybe better, without you. When you are out of the way, they will listen more to each other and the ensemble precision will improve.

As you rehearse, you should also try to speak less and show more. Once your ensemble is accustomed to your conducting style, you should be able to communicate everything you want with your gestures. Stopping to explain everything to your musicians is a crutch for conductors who have poor baton technique. I always enjoy conducting in foreign countries where I do not speak the language because it forces me to show everything. There, I cannot enjoy the luxury of verbal explanations. Instead, I must communicate completely with my gestures.

By conducting less, you will also encourage the group to "come to you." The ensemble's energy should meet you in the conducting strike zone at the table of sound. Never go out to them, either with your gestures or your energy. Going out to the ensemble diffuses the music making, and you will get a "spread" sound that is unfocused in quality. There will be nervousness in this sound and the group will not be able to play precisely together. Whenever I want to focus the quality of the sound, I simply conduct smaller and closer to my body. This enables the musicians to be drawn in, and the reduction in the size of the beat forces them to watch even more closely. Conduct less and they will come to you.

Establishing the Right Environment

As you conduct, learn to interpret the overall energy of your group. When a group is scattered and noisy, the rehearsal will not be productive. Do not be afraid to wait until the room is quiet before continuing. Sometimes you will have to wait longer than you feel is comfortable. Trust that it is worth the wait. Focusing the attention and energy of the group at the beginning of a rehearsal and again throughout is critically important. Most of us have been in situations where, at the dress rehearsal, suddenly everyone is paying attention, and the level of music making suddenly improves dramatically. Your goal is to establish that same level of attention at every rehearsal so that you can move your ensemble to a higher plateau of music making all the time. Waiting and demanding their full attention is necessary to accomplish this goal.

Once everyone is quiet and focused at the rehearsal, try to align yourself with how the musicians are feeling that day. Are certain players unhappy, tired, or nervous? Are there issues of mood that are going to affect the rehearsal later on? What can you do to diffuse any negative energy in the group? The presence of negative energy can eventually undermine the focus of your rehearsal; a few sincerely placed words of praise can turn a negative rehearsal into a positive one very quickly. The right work environment can motivate all players to participate to their fullest level.

A similar strategy can be utilized for concerts before you start each piece. Before raising your arms to conduct, evaluate the energy and attention level of the audience. Are they focused and ready to listen? Or are people still arriving, talking, and shifting in their seats? Be aware of what is happening in the room, both on the stage and in the audience, before you start. Wait to begin until everyone is ready. Just as you would never want to take a cake out of the oven until it is done, or eat a piece of fruit that is not ripe, do not start conducting until both groups, the audience and the ensemble, are ready to focus fully on the music.

HELP OTHERS BECOME SUCCESSFUL

A good conductor motivates his or her ensemble members, offering them opportunities to excel and ways to continually derive satisfaction from what they are doing. Look for chances to showcase individual musicians and be generous with your praise and encouragement. If you can help others to be successful with their careers, they will be more supportive of your own goals.

A good artistic leader does not waste time criticizing others. Even though musicians love to gossip and tell stories, it is important to remember that you are the role model for your group. You should be everyone's champion and exude a positive energy that inspires everyone's best performance. Try to "fly above the clouds" or "take the higher road." Do not allow yourself to become bogged down with critical or negative thinking. Your own reputation will increase naturally if you are positive and encouraging to the members of your ensemble.

LEADERSHIP

Strong, consistent leadership is valued by the members of your ensemble. They want to know where they stand and what the rules are. They also want to be treated fairly, consistently, and with respect. Make sure that you clarify your rules and expectations at the beginning of your tenure with your group. This will make everything easier for you later.

Flexibility—the Secret of Success

Flexibility is one of the most important attributes for any leader. Consider how a small tree might sway in a big storm, but trees that are too large to sway may fall or break because they are not flexible. Do not be like the large tree, or the dinosaur that has lived past its time. Rigidity can stifle creativity and greatly limit how people relate to you. Inflexible people are never as successful as they could be. Be flexible, like a young tree, as you are working through difficult situations with your organization.

TIMING

Timing in addressing situations in a performing ensemble is also very important. Learn to recognize problems with individual players and address them before they become larger issues. Every difficult situation usually starts from something small and simple. Learn to identify the signs of difficult issues before they get out of hand, and never assume they will go away on their own.

It is important to deal with people and situations individually so that you can find out from the person involved exactly what is wrong. Often the root of the problem is totally different from what you expected and sometimes just talking about the problem is enough to solve it.

Often, during a private conversation, musicians will present suggestions and solutions to points of conflict. When this occurs, be careful not to argue, contradict, or immediately express your own views on the matter. Instead, be a sounding board and ask more questions to clarify what the other person is saying. Many times, people just want to be heard and recognized, even if they know it will not change the final outcome of a situation.

CHOOSE YOUR BATTLES

A gentler, more flexible style of working with people will always make you more successful in the long run. When you remove yourself from the conflict, the resistance relaxes because it no longer has a target. Often, if you back down, a person will come around to your way of thinking, or at a minimum the conflict will ease, and both of you will be able to move forward in a more positive manner.

In life, there are times to stand your ground and times to retreat. I always say *"choose your battles carefully."* You do not want to win one battle at the risk of losing the entire war. Most of us learn this the hard way. Try not to draw lines in the sand on any issue and allow others to participate in the decision-making process. When we remain flexible, outcomes are often more favorable.

Declining to fight every little issue does not mean you care less about the long-term growth and development of the ensemble; it is just that some battles involve spending excessive energy in the wrong direction. Even if you win your specific battle, it is often not worth the loss of time and respect of the group, or the fracturing of the group's positive energy.

Career Development

When dealing with your conducting career, there are many times when you must wait patiently to see what comes into your life. Conducting is a very competitive field, and it takes a lifetime to master. Do not waste time or energy being depressed over jobs you have lost, or mistakes that you might have made in rehearsals or concerts. All of this is part of the learning process. Be thankful for these wonderful opportunities to learn, grow, and improve. Sometimes, when you are feeling the most vulnerable, you are actually poised to move up to the next level. We all must experience failure in order to learn. When someone feels that his or her career is not moving forward the way the person believes it should, I always say *"double your rate of failure."* Only through trying, failing, adjusting, and trying again do we eventually learn what is necessary to succeed.

BUILD YOUR NETWORK

It is important for you to become active with the various national support organizations and to build your circle of contacts in the field. It is easy to stay in touch with people now because of internet social networking sites and cell phones. Allocate some time each day to strengthening your relationship with people you know and to building and developing new relationships. Often, your next conducting position will materialize as a result of someone you know or a person who knows someone that you know.

BE OPEN TO NEW OPPORTUNITIES

There is an old saying: "*When you desire nothing, a great deal comes to you.*" I think this refers to expectations. When you release those rigid expectations of yourself, you are more open to all the possible opportunities that might come your way, and you derive more enjoyment from life. Never feel disappointed because certain expectations were not met within your specified time frame. Instead, just strive to do your best work, and remain open to whatever happens. Conductors, by their very nature, want to control everything. Try letting go of this control and see how much easier life becomes. With this mindset, I think you will ultimately achieve more.

PERSEVERE

Often it is not the person with the great musical talent who succeeds, but the one who simply perseveres. One fact is certain—if you are going to succeed as a conductor, you must remain in the field. All too often, people leave the field when difficult issues arise. Remember that life is about the journey, not the finish line. The important thing is to bring your best to your current conducting situation; to learn and grow from it; and to live in the moment. Watch and learn from other conductors and musicians who are successful in what they do, and be thankful for your own opportunities to learn and grow.

BE HUMBLE

As you reach various levels of success in the music field, refrain from gloating, or bragging. Fame is fleeting. Remember, the ladder of success goes easily in both directions, and the music industry is very small. Over the course of your career, you will run into the same people over and over, and you will probably change jobs many times. Strive to build strong lifelong relationships with those in the field because you may work with them again, or someone may ask them for a recommendation on your work. No one likes a braggart, so remember to be humble in all of your dealings with people. They will respect you more as a colleague.

BE CENTERED, CONFIDENT, AND CONSISTENT

Too often, conductors are overcommitted individuals who have no quiet time and no personal life. It is important to reserve time for yourself in your busy schedule. A musical leader who is calm, centered, and grounded will be able to work with a variety of difficult personalities successfully. A centered person is also able to evaluate difficult situations calmly, even while things are changing quickly. These types of leaders take the time to think through each problem before responding, and they are not subject to inconsistent emotional reactions. Reserve some quiet time in your schedule on a daily basis and practice the breathing exercises in Chapter 6. This will help you to remain centered and calm.

It is also important to free yourself from the influence of other people's negative thoughts about you and your work. People will always have an opinion. They might say you are too short, too tall, too fat, too thin, not smart enough, not talented enough, not musical enough, not the one they are looking for. To be a conductor, you must acquire a very thick skin to block out this criticism. It is essential that you maintain your focus on your own personal goals and the music.

PUTTING IT ALL TOGETHER

The art of conducting is a lifelong pursuit, and one that I believe can never be fully mastered as there is always something more to learn. When you are preparing for a career as a conductor, three basic areas require focus: (1) the in-depth study of the music; (2) the mastery of the gestures that communicate the music; and (3) the sensitivity to group dynamics and motivational aspects involved with inspiring large groups of people.

In this book, I have touched on all three ideas, but I have focused mostly on the concepts of *gesture* and the muscle flexibility required to develop a solid technique for communicating the music to the musicians.

Many conductors envision wonderful musical concepts but lack the technique to convey their ideas to the musicians. Often, conductors get in their own way, sending conflicting signals on what they really want. Still other conductors lead while holding a tremendous amount of stress and tension in their bodies, which negatively affects the sound quality of the music. I hope that the exercises in this book have opened up your mind to a new way of thinking about how you align your body and how your conducting gestures affect the musicians in front of you.

Training your body is an ongoing process. You will need to practice constantly, just as an athlete prepares for a race or sport, or a ballerina trains to dance. Going through the book once is not enough to train your muscles and keep them in shape. You will need to revisit these ideas regularly and practice the exercises as a daily warm-up routine.

If you do this, you will notice a tremendous difference in your conducting. You will be more relaxed, more focused, more centered, and more intuitive. Musical ideas in your head will be able to come out through your hands in ways that you never imagined possible. You will be able to make the music come to life. Your musicians will play better and they will enjoy performing with you. The level of overall musicianship will increase dramatically, and everyone will enjoy the rehearsals and concerts more.

In the end, you will be a better conductor. Your music making will be more exciting and inspiring. This is a noble goal, and one that we all would like to achieve. Gaining it requires time and diligent practice. Training your muscles and your mind will not happen overnight, but with careful preparation and study, I know you will experience dramatic results. Mastering the gestures and concepts presented in this book will change your conducting, and it will change your life. I know it changed mine.

APPENDIX

Conducting Relaxation Exercises

The Feet
- Feet Placement Chart
- Weight Shifts
- Ankle Rotations

Grounding the Lower Body
- Tiptoes Up and Down
- Leg Kicks
- Leg Swings
- Jump in Place
- Knee Bends
- Sit, Then Stand

The Waist and the Back
- Waist Swivels
- Side Bends
- Buttocks Squeeze
- Back Bend & Vertebrae Alignment
  - Releasing the Back
  - Releasing More Tension
  - Coming Back Up
  - Imaginary Shower
- Releasing the Lower Back
- Flat on the Floor
- Stand Against a Wall

Lifting the Rib Cage & Opening the Chest
- Hands Behind Your Head
- Chicken Wings
- Towel Pull
- Arm Lifts
- Windshield Wipers

The Head
- Puppet String
- Head Rolls
- Chin Placement
- Book on the Head

The Shoulders
- Arm Circles
- Shoulder Lifts
- Nuzzle the Kitten
- Shoulder and Arm Releases
- Go-Away Motion
- Falling Arms

The Arms
- Circular Placement
- Elbow Space
- Accordion Push and Pull
- Wipe the Table
- Polish the Table

The Wrist and Fingers
- Coin on Hand
- Wrist Flicks
- Wrist Finger Taps
- Wrist Circles
- Finger Drumming
- Finger Contractions

The Face and Eyes
- Face Scrunches
- Jaw Drop
- Placement of Tongue
- Mouth and Lips
- Eye Blinks
- Smiling Eyes
- Field of Vision
- Eye Contact

Conducting Diagram Charts

Standard Conducting Diagrams

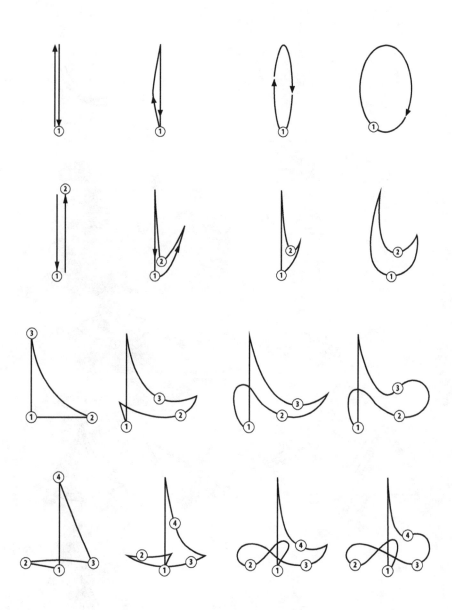

Saito Conducting Diagrams

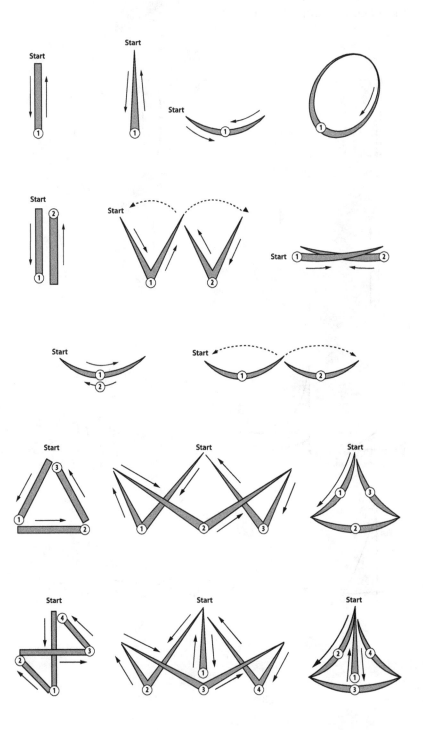

Musin Conducting Diagrams

Standard Pattern - All in One Place

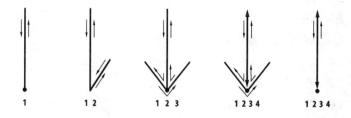

Saito Pattern - All in One Place

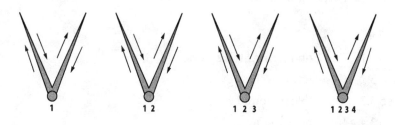

VIDEO LIST

Chapter 1:

Video 1.1   The Feet

Video 1.2   Grounding the Lower Body

Video 1.3   The Waist and the Back

Video 1.4   Lifting the Rib Cage and Opening the Chest

Video 1.5   The Head

Video 1.6   The Shoulders

Video 1.7   The Arms

Video 1.8   The Wrist and Fingers

Video 1.9   The Face and Eyes

Chapter 2:

Video 2.1   Direction

Video 2.2   Size

Video 2.3   Weight and Resistance

Video 2.4   Impact and Release

Video 2.5   The Downward Gesture

Video 2.6   The Upward Gesture

Video 2.7   Weight

Video 2.8   Sideways Gestures

Video 2.9   Motions Outward

Video 2.10 Motions Inward

Video 2.11 Circles, Arcs, and Free Motions

Video 2.12 Preparatory Beats

Chapter 3:

Video 3.1   The Conducting Strike Zone

Video 3.2   Connecting to Energy

Video 3.3   The Table of Sound

Video 3.4   Imaginary Piano

Video 3.5   Conducting with the Hand

Video 3.6   Table Taps

Video 3.7   Pencil Baton

Video 3.8   Holding the Baton
Video 3.9   Developing Your Muscles
Video 3.10 Baton Taps
Video 3.11 Standard Conducting Diagrams
Video 3.12 Ilya Musin Conducting Diagrams
Video 3.13 Hideo Saito Conducting Diagrams
Video 3.14 Subdivided Beat Patterns
Video 3.15 Merging Gestures
Video 3.16 Other Gestures
Video 3.17 The Left Hand

Chapter 4:
Video 4.1   Prep for Beat One
Video 4.2   Prep for Beat Two
Video 4.3   Prep for Beat Three
Video 4.4   Prep for Beat Four
Video 4.5   Two Prep Beats
Video 4.6   Articulated Entrances
Video 4.7   Smooth Entrances
Video 4.8   Pressed Entrances
Video 4.9   Accents
Video 4.10 Cuing Motions
Video 4.11 Cutoffs
Video 4.12 Rests
Video 4.13 Recitative
Video 4.14 Fermatas

Chapter 5:
Video 5.1   Accelerando
Video 5.2   Conducting Merged Beats
Video 5.3   Rallentando
Video 5.4   Conducting Subdivisions
Video 5.5   Conducting Individual Beats
Video 5.6   Showing Dynamics
Video 5.7   Changing Dynamics

Video 5.8   Phrasing
Video 5.9   Sudden Dynamic Changes

Useful Links and Resources

Baton Makers

National Baton Company
Email: info@batonz.com
Website: www.batonz.com
Phone: (248) 895-7894

Conrad Batons
Email: salesinfo@conradbatons.com
Website: www.conradbatons.com

Custom Batons
Email: info@custom-batons.com
Website: www.custom-batons.com
Phone: (763) 439-7432

Garrett Music Products
Email: rgarrett@iwu.edu
Website: www.garrettmusicproducts.com
Phone: (309) 556-3268

Guy Lake Custom Batons
Email: glcustombatons@yahoo.com
Website: www.glcustombatons.com
Phone: (760) 391-3484

Mollard Conducting Batons
Email: info@mollard.com
Website: www.mollard.com
Phone: (800) 842-2866
Phone: (330) 659-7081

Music Works Custom Batons
Email: order@musicworkscustombatons.com
Website: www.musicworkscustombatons.com
Phone: (303) 322-4560

Newland Custom Batons

Email: batons@newlandbatons.com

Website: www.newlandbatons.com

Phone: (800) 272-6561

Old World Baton

Email: shop@oldworldmusicandgifts.com

Website: www.oldworldbaton.com

Phone: (903) 283-2586

PaGu Batons

Website: www.pagubatons.com

Phone: (716) 200-6518

Pierce Conducting Batons

Email: piercebatons@aol.com

Website: www.alanpierceconductingbatons.com

Premier Batons L.L.C.

Email: premierbatons@cableone.net

Website: www.premierbatons.com

Phone: (800) 998-1737

Texas Batons

Email: brian@texasbatons.com

Other Email: amy@texasbatons.com

Website: www.texasbatons.com

BOOK RECOMMENDATIONS

CONDUCTING BOOKS

Del Mar, Norman. *The Anatomy of the Orchestra*. Berkeley: University of California Press, 1963.

Farberman, Harold. *The Art of Conducting Technique*. Miami, FL: Warner Brothers, 1997.

Fennell, Frederick. *A Conductor's Interpretive Analysis of Masterworks for Band*. Delray Beach, FL: Meredith Music, 2008.

Green, Elizabeth A. H. and Mark Gibson. *The Modern Conductor*, 7th ed. Upper Saddle River, NJ: Prentice Hall, 1997.

Hunsberger, Donald and Roy E. Ernst. *The Art of Conducting*. New York: McGraw-Hill, 1992.

Jordan, James. *The Conductor's Gesture: A Practical Application of Rudolf Von Laban's Movement Language*. Chicago, IL: GIA Publications, 2011.

Koshak, John. *The Conductor's Role*, 5th ed. Chapman, CA. Available from the Conductors Guild. 719 Twinridge Lane, Richmond, VA 23235

Lamb, Gordon. *Choral Techniques*. Dubuque, IA: William C. Brown, 1988.

Leinsdorf, Eric. *The Composer's Advocate*. New Haven, CT: Yale University Press, 1981.

Meier, Gustav. *The Score, the Orchestra, and the Conductor*. New York: Oxford University Press, 2009.

Rudolf, Max. *The Grammar of Conducting*, 3rd ed. New York: G Schirmer, 1995.

Saito, Hideo. *The Saito Conducting Method*. Translated by Fumihiko Torigai, edited by Wayne J. Toews. Tokyo, Japan: Min-On Concert Association and Ongaku No Tomo Sha Corp., 1988.

Schuller, Gunther. *The Compleat Conductor*. New York: Oxford University Press, 1997.

MUSIC REPERTOIRE BOOKS

Daniels, David. *Orchestral Music—a Handbook*. Lanham, MD: Scarecrow Press, 2005.

Green, Jonathan. *A Conductor's Guide to Choral-Orchestral Works, Classical Period*. Lanham, MD: Scarecrow Press, 2002.

Green, Jonathan. *A Conductor's Guide to Nineteenth-Century Choral-Orchestral Works*. Lanham, MD: Scarecrow Press, 2007.

Green, Jonathan. *A Conductor's Guide to Choral-Orchestral Works, Twentieth Century*. Lanham, MD: Scarecrow Press, 1998.

Manning, Lucy. *Orchestral Pops Music: A Handbook*. Lanham, MD: Scarecrow Press, 2009.

Meyer, Dirk. *Chamber Orchestra and Ensemble Repertoire*, Lanham, MD: Scarecrow Press, 2011.

Nicholson, Chad. *Great Music for Wind Band: A Guide to the Top 100 Works in Grades IV, V, VI*. Delray Beach, FL: Meredith Music, 2009.

Shrock, Dennis. *Choral Repertoire*. New York: Oxford University Press, 2009.

Strimple, Nick. *Choral Music in the Twentieth Century*. Portland, OR: Amadeus Press, 2005.

Votta, Michael, editor. *The Wind Band and Its Repertoire: Two Decades of Research as Published in the CBDNA Journal*. Van Nuys, CA: Alfred Music, 2006.

Yaffe, John and David Daniels. *Arias, Ensembles, & Choruses: An Excerpt Finder for Orchestras*. Lanham, MD: Scarecrow Press, 2011.

MUSIC REFERENCE BOOKS

Ammer, Christine. *The A to Z of Foreign Musical Terms*. Boston, MA: ECS Publishing, 1989.

Caroll, Raynor. *Symphonic Repertoire Guide for Timpani and Percussion*. Pasadena, CA: Batterie Music, 2005 (distributed by Carl Fischer).

Girsberger, Russ. *A Practical Guide to Percussion Terminology*. Fort Lauderdale, FL: Meredith Music, 1998.

Girsberger, Russ and Laurie Lake. *The Music Performance Library: A Practical Guide for Orchestra, Band and Opera Librarians.* Delray Beach, FL: Meredith Music, 2011.
Wittry, Diane. *Beyond the Baton: What Every Conductor Needs to Know.* New York: Oxford University Press, 2007.

Motivational Books

Zander, Benjamin and Rosamund Stone Zander. *The Art of Possibility.* Boston, MA: Harvard Business School Press, 2000.

Leadership Books

Baker, William F. and Michael O'Malley. *Leading with Kindness.* New York: American Management Association, 2008.
Blanchard, Kenneth. *The One Minute Manager.* New York: Berkley Books, 1982.
Collins, Jim. *Good to Great—Why Some Companies Make the Leap.* New York: Harper Collins, 2001.
Covey, Stephen R. *First Things First.* New York: Simon and Schuster, 1994.
Covey, Stephen R. *The Seven Habits of Highly Effective People.* New York: Simon and-Schuster, 1989.
Ferrazzi, Keith and Tahl Raz. *Never Eat Alone: And Other Secrets to Success, One Relationship at a Time.* New York: Doubleday, 2005.

Nonprofit Management

Hinsley, Matthew. *Creativity to Community—Arts Nonprofit Success One Coffee at a Time.* Austin, TX: Envision Arts, 2010.
Kaiser, Michael M. *The Art of the Turnaround: Creating and Maintaining Healthy Arts Organization.* Waltham, MA: University of New England, 2008.
Korza, Pam, editor. *Fundamentals of Arts Management,* 5th ed. (first published in 1987 as *Fundamentals of Local Arts Management*). Amherst, MA: Arts Extension Service, 2007.
Woodward, Jeannette. *Nonprofit Essentials: Managing Technology.* Hoboken, NJ: John Wiley, 2006.

Fundraising and Grants

Burnett, Ken. *Relationship Fundraising—A Donor-Based Approach to the Business of Raising Money,* 2nd ed. San Francisco, CA: White Lion Press, 2002.
Carlson, Mim. *Winning Grants: Step by Step, the Complete Workbook for Planning, Developing, and Writing Successful Proposals.* San Francisco, CA: John Wiley, 2008.
Hopkins, Karen Brooks and Carolyn Stolper Friedman. *Successful Fundraising for Arts and Cultural Organizations,* 2nd ed. Westport, CT: Oryx Press, 1997.
Kiritz, Norton J. *Program Planning and Proposal Writing.* Grantsmanship Center, 2007 (pamphlet).

Marketing and Social Media

Bettger, Frank. *How I Raised Myself from Failure to Success in Selling.* New York: Prentice-Hall, 1986.

Carr, Eugene. *Wired for Culture: How E-mail Is Revolutionizing Arts Marketing,* 3rd ed. New York: Patron Publishing, 2007.

Carr, Eugene. *Sign-Up for Culture: The Arts Marketer's Guide to Building an Effective E-mail List.* New York: Patron Publishing, 2004.

Cialdini, Robert B. *Influence, the Psychology of Persuasion.* New York: Collins Business Essentials, 1984.

Gillin, Paul. *The New Influencers: A Marketer's Guide to the New Social Media.* Fresno, CA: Quill Driver Books, 2009.

Gladwell, Malcolm. *The Tipping Point: How Little Things Can Make a Big Difference.* New York: Little, Brown, 2002.

Godin, Seth. *Purple Cow—Transform Your Business by Being Remarkable.* New York: Portfolio (published by the Penguin Group), 2002.

Kotler, Philip and Joanne Scheff. *Standing Room Only: Strategies for Marketing the Performing Arts.* Cambridge, MA: Harvard Business School Press, 1997.

Scott, David Meerman. *The New Rules of Marketing & PR: How to Use News Releases, Blogs, Podcasting, Viral Marketing & Online Media to Reach Buyers Directly.* Hoboken, NJ: David Wiley. 2009.

Sernovitz, Andy. *Word of Mouth Marketing: How Smart Companies Get People Talking.* New York: Kaplan, 2006.

Music Organizations

American Bandmasters Association (ABA)
Email: wmoody4250@att.net
Website: www.americanbandmasters.org

American Choral Directors Association (ACDA)
Email: membership@acda.org
Website: www.acda.org
Phone: (405) 232-8161

American School Band Directors Association (ASBDA)
Email: spluess@frontier.com
Website: www.asbda.com
Phone: (555) 252-2500

American String Teachers Association (ASTA)
Email: asta@astaweb.com
Website: www.astaweb.com
Phone: (703) 279-2113

Association of Concert Bands (ACB)
Email: president@acbands.org
Website: www.acbands.org
Phone: (800) 726-8720

Chorus America
Email: service@chorusamerica.org
Website: www.chorusamerica.org
Phone: (202) 331-7577

College Band Directors National Association (CBDNA)
Email: thomas.verrier@vanderbilt.edu
Website: www.cbdna.org
Phone: (615) 322-7651

College Orchestra Directors Association (CODA)
Email: kbartram@umw.edu
Website: codaweb.org
Phone: (540) 654-1956

Conductors Guild
Email: guild@conductorsguild.org
Website: www.conductorsguild.org
Phone: (804) 553-1378

International Federation for Choral Music (IFCM)
Email: Office@ifcm.net
Website: www.ifcm.net

League of American Orchestra (LAO)
Email: league@americanorchestras.org
Website: www.americanorchestras.org
Phone: (212) 262-5161

National Association for Music Educators (NAfME)
Email: memberservices@nafme2.org
Website: www.nafme.org
Phone: (703) 860 -4000

National Association of Music Merchants (NAMM)
Email: info@namm.org
Website: www.namm.org
Phone: (760) 438-8001

National Band Association (NBA)
Email: info@nationalbandassociation.org
Website: www.nationalbandassociation.org

National Collegiate Choral Organization (NCCO)
Email: contact@ncco-usa.org
Website: www.ncco-usa.org

Opera America
Email: Info@operaamerica.org
Website: www.operaamerica.org
Phone: (212) 796-8620

OTHER WEBSITES

Alexander Technique
www.alexandertechnique.com

Alexander Technique Educational Center
www.alexandertechnique.org

Alexander Method
www.alexandermethod.com

American Society for Alexander Teaching
www.amsatonline.org

Classical Singer
www.Classicalsinger.com

Conducting Master Classes
www.conductingmasterclass.wordpress.com

Choral Net
www.choralnet.org

Laban Guild for Movement and Dance
www.labanguild.org.uk

Music Chairs
www.musicalchairs.info

National Qigong Association (NQA)
www.nqa.org

Pilates Certification
www.pilatescertificationonline.com

Pilates Method Alliance (PMA)
www.pilatesmethodalliance.org

Singers
www.Singers.com

Website Conducting Examples:

Reuben Blundell
Music Director, Hunter Symphony, New York
Conductor, The Chelsea Symphony

Gemma New
Associate Conductor, New Jersey Symphony
Music Director, Lunar Ensemble

Michael Avagliano
Music Director and Conductor
Central Jersey Symphony

Rick Peckham
Videographer, Video Editing, Diagrams and Illustrations

CPSIA information can be obtained
at www.ICGtesting.com
Printed in the USA
BVHW080203120222
628033BV00002B/9

9 780199 354160